PISTOLS AND POINTED PENS

The Field of Honor
—*Richmond Newspapers*

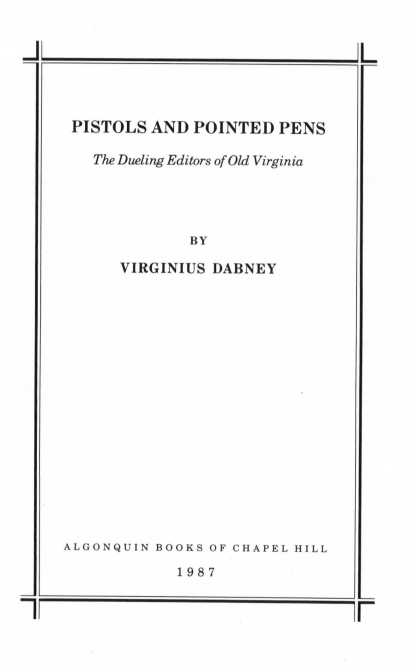

PISTOLS AND POINTED PENS

The Dueling Editors of Old Virginia

BY

VIRGINIUS DABNEY

ALGONQUIN BOOKS OF CHAPEL HILL

1987

Published by
Algonquin Books of Chapel Hill
Post Office Box 2225
Chapel Hill, North Carolina 27515-2225

in association with
Taylor Publishing Company
1550 West Mockingbird Lane
Dallas, Texas 75235

Design by Molly Renda

LIBRARY OF CONGRESS CATALOGING-IN-PUBLICATION DATA
Dabney, Virginius, 1901–
Pistols and pointed pens.

"Published . . . in association with Taylor Publishing
Company"—Verso t.p.
Bibliography: p.
1. American newspapers—Virginia—Richmond—History—
19th century. 2. Journalists—Virginia—Richmond—
Biography. I. Title.
PN4899.R53D3 1987 070.4′1′0922 [B] 87-12547
ISBN 0-912697-70-9

This book is dedicated to
Lewis Franklin Powell, Junior
A great justice of the United States Supreme Court
An illustrious Virginian
and a cherished friend

CONTENTS

LIST OF ILLUSTRATIONS

LIST OF ILLUSTRATIONS

Judge John C. Underwood
Richmond *Dispatch* building, Twelfth and Main
General William Mahone
Charles T. O'Ferrall
John Mercer Langston
William C. Elam
William E. Cameron
J. G. (Parson) Massey
John Hampden Chamberlayne
Carter Glass
John Mitchell, Jr.
Richmond *Planet* for December 14, 1907
Richmond *Times* front page for February 16, 1898
Richmond *Times* building, Tenth and Bank
Statue of Joseph Bryan, Monroe Park

ACKNOWLEDGMENTS

I am indebted to many persons for assistance in the preparation of this book. Louis D. Rubin, Jr., president of Algonquin Books of Chapel Hill, suggested the subject and aided me greatly along the way. The accommodating and efficient staff at the Virginia State Library was always helpful—notably, Diane Pettway, Andrea Brown, Kay McCall, Minor Weisiger, Paulette Thomas, and Bradwill Wilson. At the Virginia Historical Society, Virginius Hall, Jr., and Frances Fugate were wholly cooperative, as usual, while the same may be said of Kathy Albers at Richmond Newspapers and William Simpson at the Richmond Public Library. Mrs. Henry M. Cowardin and Edwin M. Cowardin, Jr., aided me materially with information concerning the Cowardins, while George Crutchfield at the Virginia Commonwealth University School of Mass Communications has placed me in his debt, as has Bernard J. Henley.

The Virginia editor is a young, unmarried, intemperate, pugnacious gambling gentleman. Between drink and dueling-
pistols he is generally escorted to a premature grave. If he so far
withstands the ravages of brandy and gunpowder as to reach the
period of gray hairs and cautiousness, he is deposed to make
room for a youth who hates his life with an utter hatred and who
can't keep drunk for more than a week at a time."

Thus wrote Dr. George W. Bagby, himself a Virginia editor, in
the 1850s. A graceful and humorous commentator on the passing
scene in Virginia both before and after the Civil War, Bagby produced a classic essay on "The Virginia Editor." He obviously indulged in a few "stretchers," but it contained more than a few
grains of truth.

Virginia editors in the antebellum and postbellum eras, by
and large, were a bellicose lot, and they faced a constant threat of
challenge to the so-called field of honor. Whenever the editorial

writer took his pen in hand, he did so with full awareness that he might be risking his life.

Thomas Ritchie, the editor of the Richmond *Enquirer* for forty-one years, was perhaps the most influential editorial pundit of them all. A power in the Democratic party for decades, "Father" Ritchie's endorsement for public office was understood to be worth thousands of votes. Virginians who left the state for the Deep South, as many did, were said to read Ritchie's editorials in the *Enquirer*, or those of his great rival John Hampden Pleasants in the Richmond *Whig*, so as to keep in close touch with the Virginia version of Reality. The slashing commentaries of John M. Daniel, editor of the Richmond *Examiner* before and during the Civil War, made him widely feared and even hated, but he was read. There were others of almost equal stature.

The fury and violence of the language used by many of these editors was almost incredible, especially when one considers the extreme risks that they ran in so expressing themselves. "Cowardly liar," "consummate traitor," "conceited ass" and "contemptible scoundrel" were only a few of the epithets that they hurled at one another, or at random persons with whom they disagreed, regardless of the consequences.

Party newspapers came into being in the early years of the century, and thereafter the spirit of party contributed to the vitality as well as the malignity of the press. In the early years of the republic, political parties had been unknown. When Thomas Jefferson returned from France in 1789, he had no intention of founding a political party, and he remarked: "If I could not go to heaven but with a party, I would not wish to go there at all." No provision for parties was contained in the U.S. Constitution, and George Washington hoped to get along without them.

But in the early 1790s Thomas Jefferson and James Madison, disturbed at what they considered the anti-French, antidemocratic influence of Alexander Hamilton and his supporters, persuaded the poet Philip Freneau, Madison's classmate at Princeton, to come to Philadelphia, then the nation's capital, and start an opposition paper. Thus the seeds were planted for the Jeffersonian Republican party and its successors. At about the same time the Federalist party was formed around Alexander Hamilton and his supporters. By the time of Andrew Jackson's presidency the division of the electorate into Democrats and Whigs was just about complete.

Partisanship in the press was greatly enhanced by the founding of political parties. Party newspapers made little pretense to fairness in addressing public questions. Consider the observations of the Philadelphia *Aurora* upon the administration of George Washington when he retired from the presidency in 1797. Washington, the indispensable man who had led us to victory in the Revolution and then served as first president of the infant republic, was termed, incredibly, "the source of all the misfortunes of our country." The organ of the Republicans went on to say that "it is the subject of the greatest astonishment that a single individual should have carried his designs against the public liberty so far as to put in jeopardy its very existence."

This diatribe was matched by that of the Federalist New England *Palladium*, which delivered itself of the dictum that "should the infidel Thomas Jefferson be elected to the presidency, the seal of death is that moment set on our holy religion, our churches will be prostrated, and some infamous prostitute, under the title of the Goddess of Reason, will preside in the sanctuaries now devoted to the most high." Such scurrilous nonsense was published frequently during the first third of the nineteenth century, and while there was improvement in later years, there continued to be much vigor and no little vituperation in editorial pronouncements.

Thomas Jefferson, a major sufferer at the hands of journalists, said in 1807 that "nothing can now be believed which is seen in a newspaper." Nevertheless, he stated near the end of his life that "the only security of all is in a free press." George Wythe, his contemporary, declared that "the occupation of newspaper editors had become lower than that of scavengers; the former brought filth into our streets, the latter cleansed them."

The code duello was then in full force, and political differences swiftly became personal affronts, to be settled with pistol and ball. Several distinguished journalists of the Old Dominion were killed in duels. John Hampden Pleasants, the brilliant editor of the Richmond *Whig*, was the most conspicuous of these, and those of his compatriots who survived "pistols at ten paces" often had close calls. Young and recklessly brave O. Jennings Wise, editor of the Richmond *Enquirer* just before the Civil War, fought eight duels in two years. Nobody was killed in his confrontations, and Wise came through them unscathed, only to be slain when serving with the Richmond Light Infantry Blues in the Confederate defeat at Roanoke Island in 1862.

There were laws against dueling, subjecting those who killed their adversaries to charges of murder, but it was almost impossible to get convictions. Juries were unwilling to return verdicts of guilty for those who defended their "honor" in this fashion. Duels were fought only with those deemed to be one's social equals. If one were insulted by a person not regarded as occupying the requisite level of social prominence, a horsewhipping or caning was felt to be in order.

The reductio ad absurdum of the code duello seems to have occurred at the Virginia Military Institute in the 1850s, when a senior cadet, James A. Walker, challenged Professor Thomas J. Jackson, later the immortal "Stonewall," when Jackson reprimanded him for misbehavior in class. Walker was court-martialed and expelled. He later commanded the Stonewall Brigade, and was awarded his degree by VMI after the war.

Dueling was just as prevalent in the Deep South as in Virginia.

A visitor to Savannah at the end of the eighteenth century found seven duels scheduled for a single day in that vicinity. More than a hundred such encounters occurred in Georgia during the nineteenth century.

There was a tradition of violence in Virginia and the rest of the South which contributed to this overall situation. Living on farms or plantations, accustomed to hunting and handling guns, active in the out-of-doors and addicted to field sports, Southerners were independent individualists who tended to take situations into their own hands. The South's martial tradition was another important element in shaping characters. Southerners were leaders and fighters in all the country's wars, from the French and Indian War through the American Revolution, the War of 1812, and the Civil War.

The South's tradition of violence seems to have extended to the fair sex in one border state, although not in the South proper, as far as is known. J. B. Jones records in his *Rebel War Clerk's Diary* that in 1864 "great excitement was produced in the House of Representatives this morning by the entrance of a lady who proceeded vigorously to cowhide the Hon. Mr. V—— from Missouri." This Amazon appears to have been far ahead of her time. Even the most militant and bellicose modern advocates of women's rights have not yet taken to flogging our statesmen in the halls of Congress.

Virginia journalism had its origins with William Parks, a native Englishman who came to Maryland and established the *Maryland Gazette* in 1727. After several years, he moved to Williamsburg and launched the *Virginia Gazette* in 1736, a paper which reached a high level of excellence for the time. Governor William Berkeley of Virginia had previously made himself more or less immortal in 1671 by saying: "I thank God there are no free schools nor printing in Virginia, and I hope we shall not have these hundred years; for learning has brought disobedience and heresy and sects into the world, and printing has divulged them, and libels against the government. God keep us from both!"

Crusty old Berkeley was long since gone when Parks arrived in the colony to establish a paper. Newspapers in that day were essentially printing jobs, for their proprietors did not take editorial positions on public questions, or seek to promote the fortunes of this or that candidate for public office. It was not until the party press appeared some three-quarters of a century later that editors everywhere in the United States began choosing up sides and enlisting under the banner of the Republicans or the Federalists.

But if the *Virginia Gazette* did not seek to guide public opinion, it endeavored to present the news, both "foreign and domestick." It was also a pioneer in the use of advertising. Parks, furthermore, encouraged literary endeavor in his newspaper, and he published significant works of poetry and prose in books that were exceptionally attractive in format and design.

News of the colony was stressed in the *Gazette*, and when ships arrived bearing tidings from overseas, Parks published these as "the freshest advices." The intelligence they communicated was weeks if not months old, but the press of that day had no means of getting foreign news except via slow-moving sailing vessels.

By the standards of the time, the *Gazette* was attractive typographically, but the type in all newspapers was frightfully small and hard to read, especially since candles furnished the only nighttime illumination. Since most papers consisted of only four pages, every effort was made to cram as much material as possible into them. Minuscule type continued to be used until the end of the nineteenth century and to a lesser degree into the twentieth.

When Parks died in 1750, his paper was taken over by William Hunter, who continued it for about a decade, after which there were other proprietors, and at times more than one Virginia *Gazette*. The paper went out of existence in 1779.

When the party press emerged some two decades later, a notorious participant in the journalistic controversies that it produced was James T. Callender. A native of Scotland, Callender had fled to this country in the 1790s to avoid a trial for sedition. He became active as a writer for anti-Federalist causes, and this commended him to Thomas Jefferson, with whom he collaborated from time to time.

When Jefferson became president, Callender tried to get from him the appointment of postmaster of Richmond. Jefferson refused to give him this, whereupon an infuriated Callender sought revenge by circulating in his paper, the Richmond *Recorder*, the allegation that the President had taken a Monticello slave, Sally Hemings, as his mistress and had fathered several children by her. Callender presented absolutely no evidence, and in the opinion of the principal authorities on Jefferson's career, there wasn't any. The Federalist press, nevertheless, leaped upon this juicy morsel in Callender's newspaper and spread the charges from one end of the country to the other. And that is the flimsy basis for the canard concerning Thomas Jefferson and Sally Hemings, a canard revived and spread abroad by Fawn Brodie in 1974 with her *Thomas Jefferson: An Intimate Portrait*. Like Callender, Mrs. Brodie produced no credible evidence that the charges were based on anything more substantial than rumor and gossip.

The disreputable and unscrupulous Callender, wont to gaze with undue frequency upon the wine when it was red, got drunker than usual one day in 1803, and his body was found in the James River at Richmond in three feet of water. Thus ended the ignoble career of one of this country's earliest partisan journalists.

The vicious charges that were frequently made in the early nineteenth century by organs of both the Republicans and the Federalists make the sins of today's newspapers seem mild by comparison. There appeared to be no limit to their lack of scruple and complete disregard for the truth. In addition to shamelessly disseminating falsehoods concerning the opposition, these sheets usually refused to carry replies from the person or organization they had slandered. It is to the credit of James Madison that he suggested in 1828 that party organs begin publishing "the other side" in these controversies. His proposal was without noticeable effect, however.

A newspaper could be launched in that day by anybody who had a modest sum of money, a "shirt-tail" of type, and a small press. It was therefore an era of truly personal journalism, when papers were often identified with a single individual who combined the positions of editor and publisher. This is in glaring contrast to the situation that prevails today, when millions of dollars are required to start the average daily and few cities in America can support even two competing papers.

In the pages that follow, an effort will be made to describe and appraise the careers of a group of leading Virginia journalists of the nineteenth century. Because Richmond was the state capital, what its newspapers had to say about politics was of particular importance to voters of the time, and I have centered my inquiry on the editors of those newspapers.

They were a picturesque lot. Each of them evidenced exceptional ability, and each of them had a significant impact on his day and generation. Their names were associated in the public mind with the papers they represented. They often denounced the opposition in sulphurous language, in accordance with the prevailing mores, and this not infrequently brought challenges to the dueling field. Only one of the group was killed, but several others were wounded and had narrow escapes from death. The story of these men's widely ramified careers is the story of personalities and events that helped to shape the history of Virginia.

By the time that I became a part of Richmond's journalistic scene in the 1920s, things had quieted down considerably insofar as virtuoso editorial performance was concerned. As editor of the *Times-Dispatch*, certain of my political and social opinions doubtless aroused the ire of local citizenry from time to time, as did those of my counterpart on the *News Leader*, the late Douglas Southall Freeman, but happily it was not expected of either of us that we defend the integrity of our commentary with dueling pistols. For that, as for many other aspects of journalism as a vocation in my own day, I am grateful.

Richmond, Virginia   VIRGINIUS DABNEY
January 1, 1987

CHAPTER ONE

THOMAS RITCHIE AND THE *ENQUIRER*

I read but a single newspaper, Ritchie's *Enquirer*," Thomas Jefferson wrote in 1823, "the best that has been or is published in America."

Thomas Ritchie, who spoke through the columns of the Richmond *Enquirer* for more than forty years, was as distinguished and influential a journalistic voice for a political party as this country has produced. At age twenty-six Ritchie became the first editor of the *Enquirer*, which was founded in 1804 as an organ of the Republican (later the Democratic) party. The paper was widely recognized as reflecting the views of both Thomas Jefferson and James Madison. Ritchie achieved such renown in Virginia that a county in what is now West Virginia was named for him, and his stature on the national scene was such that he was frequently mentioned as a possible candidate for vice-president of the United States.

It was during the first four decades of the nineteenth century that the Virginia press, and in particular the Richmond newspapers, attained their greatest influence. In effect their story is that of the movement of American politics from a cleavage along economic lines to one in which slavery and sectionalism became the principal issue. Just as the expansion of the new republic into the area beyond the Appalachian Mountains and then into the trans-Mississippi territories created a rivalry for control of the Congress that ultimately saw South and North competing for dominance, so gradually the slavery issue became the principal center of editorial contention.

From being the leading journalistic voice for Jeffersonian democracy, the *Enquirer* came more and more to speak for the proslavery South, at a time when states' rights and the strict construction of the powers allocated to the national government in the Constitution were the issues that symbolized the diverging interests of North and South. Although Ritchie in the *Enquirer* opposed slavery as an institution and urged Virginia to move toward its abolition, it was the states' rights—strict construction cause that lead him to break with the Jackson administration in the late 1820s. In so doing, Ritchie aligned himself with the South as a section whose interests were focused upon the protection and expansion of slavery, and the *Enquirer* thereafter ceased largely to be the voice of the Democratic party except as its objectives coincided with those of the South.

The *Enquirer* was vigorous in expressing its opinions, though without indulging in the billingsgate and personal abuse that characterized the writings of many editors of the period. But if Ritchie refrained from calling his opponents cowards, traitors, and swine, he did not hesitate to belabor them when he felt that the occasion demanded. He also turned on several friends and associates when he believed that circumstances warranted. Although he had been a friend of both Henry Clay and John C. Calhoun, Ritchie later assailed them with such vehemence that he is

2

credited in some quarters with keeping both men from the presidency. He also broke with Martin Van Buren, whom he had previously supported.

Throughout the first half of the nineteenth century, Richmond was a Federalist, or Whig, stronghold; thus, the *Enquirer*, as a Republican-Democratic organ, was bucking the tide. John Marshall was the leading Federalist in Richmond, and the city's leaders were mainly of that political faith. A countervailing force was what was known as the Essex Junto, whose principal figures were three natives of Essex County: Ritchie, Judge Spencer Roane of the Virginia Supreme Court of Appeals, and Dr. John Brockenbrough of the Bank of Virginia.

The Essex Junto, also called the Richmond Junto, was extremely influential in Republican circles throughout Virginia, and Ritchie was its most powerful member. Judge Roane had been Jefferson's choice for chief justice of the United States, but John Adams named John Marshall to the post before Jefferson could appoint Roane. The latter was a cousin of Ritchie's, as was Dr. Brockenbrough.

Ritchie was a strong believer in the Union and also in states' rights. His views were decidedly progressive on such issues as education, agriculture, women's rights and the voting rights of citizens in western Virginia. At times, his views on slavery were remarkably liberal. As a consequence, he was regarded askance by many members of the plantation aristocracy.

Thomas Ritchie was the son of Archibald Ritchie, a native of Scotland, who came to Virginia and became a prosperous merchant and exporter. The senior Ritchie was described in some circles as a Tory in the Revolution, but in the opinion of Charles H. Ambler, to whose *Thomas Ritchie: A Study in Virginia Politics* I am greatly indebted, this is unfair. Ambler states that "Ritchie was among the last to break away from the mother country," but that "there is no evidence that he opposed the cause of the patriots after war was declared." On the contrary, records show that he furnished gunpowder free of charge to the Continental forces. All three of his sons, including Thomas, served in the War of 1812, and one was killed. Archibald Ritchie died when Thomas was only six years old, and the boy was greatly influenced by his mother. She was a Roane, and a person of culture and taste. The comfortable home in which they lived and which Archibald Ritchie built at Tappahannock, once known as "Hobbs Hole," is one of the sights there today.

Young Ritchie tried both law and medicine but was not attracted to either profession. At age twenty-one he took charge of an academy in Fredericksburg, but his health was not good, and in 1803 he came to Richmond and opened a small bookstore.

At about that time, the plant of the Richmond *Examiner* was destroyed by fire. Edited by two brothers, Meriwether and Skelton Jones, both of whom were later killed in duels, the *Examiner* was a Republican organ. When it went out of business the Republicans cast about for some means of establishing another paper representing that party in the citadel of Federalism. Jefferson and Spencer Roane prevailed upon Ritchie to become editor of the *Enquirer*, which Roane was instrumental in establishing in 1804.

The paper was a party organ to a degree seldom seen today. It received party patronage and, in effect, was underwritten by the Republicans. For nearly all of his editorship Ritchie did the state's public printing. He was entirely frank in stating that he expected to speak for the Republican administration, and that he anticipated compensation for those services. In so strong a center of Federalist sentiment as Richmond, and in competition with a well-established press, the *Enquirer* could not have survived without some form of financial support, at least at the outset.

It should be emphasized, however, that Ritchie's views were not purchased. He was an enthusiastic believer in Thomas Jefferson's program and principles. On the other hand, he was no slavish supporter, and he took issue at times with the views of the master of Monticello.

Jefferson's far-reaching and forward-looking, multifaceted program appealed to him strongly. Like Jefferson, Ritchie was convinced that the Virginia aristocracy was excessively conservative in outlook, and he sought to bring about a change. He also shared Jefferson's longtime adherence to states' rights. Another important influence on his thinking in these early years was that of Henry Clay, to whom he later became bitterly hostile.

At the outset of his editorship, Ritchie lived in what Samuel B. Mordecai described as "a plain and not spacious wooden building at the northeast corner of Franklin and Third Streets." Later he moved to "a more commodious tenement" on Grace Street between Fifth and Sixth. This was 511 East Grace, which he occupied until 1826, after which he lived at 509.

Ritchie was indefatigable in his attention to his editorial duties. Despite his many civic responsibilities, he seldom went to sleep before 3:00 A.M. "On his back, with two large candlesticks at his head, he examined exchanges and produced those editorials which shaped the political thinking of others," Ambler wrote in his biography. Yet he was punctual in arriving at his office the next morning.

For many years his slender figure was almost invariably clothed in "a white Marseilles vest, and thin pumps and silk stockings," a friend wrote, "and we have often seen him thus clad in snow and mire, in the depth of winter, wending his way homeward . . . and without an overcoat, while all others were wrapped in furs and flannels as heavy as could be worn."

He was sought after to preside at important functions of all kinds. And as the *Enquirer* said after his death:

Mr. Ritchie was the manager at all the public balls, and was the perfect gentleman in his attention to the ladies—was one of the committee of arrangements for all public dinners ... presided on those occasions with dignity and propriety. ... He welcomed public guests at public entertainments ... was a member of pleasant clubs, and none so jovial and gay as he ... never in his gayest stepping beyond the bounds of temperance and moderation.... But in his hours of study, on business or composition, he rarely permitted himself to be interrupted.

One of the guests whom Ritchie welcomed at a large dinner was Charles Dickens, the British novelist, who came to Richmond in 1842. The *Enquirer* editor's remarks were in good taste, except when he declared that Virginia had produced statesmen "who never indulged in works of the imagination, in the charms of romance, or the mere beauties of the *belles-lettres*." Since Dickens' claim to fame rested on his production of *belles lettres*, the word "mere" must have had some of the audience wincing. Dickens evidenced no displeasure at the time, but on returning to England he blasted Virginia and the South for what he termed their "gloom and dejection," and an "air of ruin and decay" wherever "slavery sits brooding."

When Aaron Burr's trial for treason occurred at Richmond in 1807, the *Enquirer* shared Jefferson's views as to Burr's guilt. Ritchie wrote:

Mr. J. Randolph may degrade Burr's *project* into an *intrigue*, intrigue of the most dangerous sort. It was executed by a man of astonishing genius; penetrating, acquainted with *man*, daring, desperate, and ambitious; by a man who was much encircled with splendid honors; and whose pecuniary means were adequate to his wants—No! it was not a mere intrigue. It was a conspiracy of the most dangerous nature. It was planned by an American Catiline; and some Sallust will hereafter record it.

The *Enquirer* also assailed John Marshall, who presided at the trial, for dining with the accused, calling this act "a reprehensible and willful prostration of his own dignity and a wanton insult to his country." The paper demanded Marshall's impeachment.

Benjamin Watkins Leigh, then a young lawyer, risked his future by attacking the chief justice in a clever series of verses, one of which follows:

> Their lot forbade; nor circumscribed alone
> Their groveling vices, but their joys confined.
> To them luxurious banquets were unknown,
> With these *poor* rogues their *judge* had never dined.

Ritchie diverged sharply from Jefferson during the events leading up to the War of 1812. When the British frigate *Leopard* attacked the American cruiser *Chesapeake* in the same year that the Burr trial took place, Ritchie was outraged. Moreover, he deserted his bride of a few weeks and marched off to Norfolk with the Republican Blues. No blood was spilled and he returned to his desk. But he soon became an ardent advocate of war with Great Britain, in complete disagreement with Jefferson. When the conflict came, he was congratulated for his part in bringing it about. He served briefly in the military, but the exact nature of his service remains obscure.

One of Ritchie's most firmly held convictions was for the maintenance of the Union. When four New England senators, led by Timothy Pickering, fought the Louisiana Purchase and threatened secession, the *Enquirer* denounced them. The Yankee legislators argued that the addition of so huge an area to the United States would draw population from New England and lessen its influence in the councils of the nation. About a decade later, during the War of 1812, the Hartford Convention was similarly toying with the idea of secession. Ritchie blasted their divisive program as "treasonable."

His record on the slavery question was not consistent, but for portions of his career he was far ahead of his time. After taking over the editorship of the *Enquirer*, he urged enactment of laws restricting the liberty of free Negroes and making it more difficult for slaves to get their freedom. But soon thereafter he was influential in securing the passage of legislation prohibiting the African slave trade after 1808, a trade which he denounced as involving "horrible crimes" against humanity. True, it appears that his advocacy of the law was motivated, in part, by the fact that the trade was cutting into the sale of surplus Virginia blacks in the Deep South. Ritchie attacked slavery as an evil but acknowledged that it was not forbidden in the Scriptures.

The Nat Turner insurrection of 1831 in Southampton County—in which some fifty-eight whites, mostly women and children, were massacred by slaves—terrified Virginians and Southerners generally, and caused them to give serious thought to abolishing or modifying the slave system. When the General Assembly met soon thereafter for its 1831–32 session, Ritchie attracted the attention of the nation by boldly proclaiming that slavery ought to be gradually abolished. Legislation calling for removal of free blacks to Africa was not enough, he declared.

"Something ought to be done," Ritchie wrote in the *Enquirer*; "means sure but gradual, systematic and discreet, ought to be adopted for reducing the mass of evil which is pressing upon the South, and will still more press upon her, the longer it is put off." Terming slavery "the black curse," he said it had seriously crippled the progress of Virginia, and he contrasted the state's condition with that prevailing in the free states of the North. Irate slaveowners canceled their subscriptions and held indignation meetings.

The freest and frankest discussion of slavery in many years followed before the General Assembly, and it appeared that something significant might be accomplished. In the end, however, the lawmakers defeated not only the plan for gradual elimination of chattel servitude but also the scheme to send to Africa those free slaves who were willing to go.

The failure of the lawmakers to act constructively was tragic in its consequences. Ritchie and his fellow liberals on the slavery issue became discouraged and the conservatives took over. Almost simultaneously, William Lloyd Garrison and his New England abolitionist cohorts became more inflammatory in their exhortations to the slaves to revolt; and Thomas R. Dew, an able thirty-year-old William and Mary professor, produced his highly influential *Essay on Slavery*. Dew argued that the "peculiar institution," far from being an evil, was a positive good and "perhaps the principal means for impelling forward the civilization of mankind." This preposterous thesis was enormously potent in influencing opinion among a Virginia population which had become greatly alarmed by the Nat Turner insurrection, and by the subsequent exhortations in Garrison's *Liberator* to other slaves to rise and slay their masters. Ritchie and many others concluded that the time was not ripe for elimination of the slave problem, since this would "leave behind it a greater, the Negro problem."

But if Ritchie's record on this issue was inconsistent, he remained staunchly progressive in such areas as extension of suffrage, promotion of public education, and development of a scientific agriculture. His forward-looking views led to a breach between him and Claiborne Gooch, coeditor of the *Enquirer* from 1820 to 1828. Gooch was a planter who owned several large estates in eastern Virginia, and his opinions on public issues diverged increasingly from those of his editorial associate. He finally resigned his position on the paper. Many of Gooch's aristocratic friends were anxious to put the *Enquirer* out of business, if possible, and they urged Gooch to establish a rival journal. He declined.

Ritchie was a strong advocate of the state constitutional convention of 1829–30, called primarily to deal with contentions from western Virginia that it was entitled to more representation in the legislature. The convention was termed "the last gathering of the giants," since aging James Madison, James Monroe, and John Marshall—all delegates—made what was expected to be their final public appearances.

Ritchie argued in his columns that there was no possible excuse for a system which made the vote of a man in Shenandoah count for only one-twelfth as much as that of a man in Gloucester. The lowlanders, he said, were maintaining an oligarchy under the guise of democracy. The franchise, he contended, should be extended to leaseholders and householders, and not be limited to freeholders, as was then the case. He was also anxious to give the West fairer representation in the General Assembly.

The franchise was extended in the manner he sought, a concession to the West, and the Shenandoah Valley and northern Piedmont received additional representation; but what is now roughly West Virginia got even fewer representatives than before. Ritchie made the best of it and accepted the outcome. Indeed, he was a major factor in achieving such progress as was made. Hugh Blair Grigsby, a member of the convention and its historian, wrote that Ritchie "sat at the clerk's table taking notes, and though not a member of the convention had more influence through the zeal and ability of his editing than any of the delegates."

The editor of the *Enquirer* was equally forward-looking in the matter of education. At first, he urged the establishment of public schools for the disadvantaged, apparently as an entering wedge for statewide public education. He supported the founding of the Lancasterian schools for the poor in Richmond, Norfolk, Alexandria, and other urban centers. Later he strongly backed a public school system for all as "the salvation of the republic." Ritchie advocated such a system before the Educational Convention at Richmond in 1842. The slaveholding aristocracy was, in general, opposed, and the public school system was not established until 1870.

The *Enquirer*'s editor was not only a staunch advocate of public schools; he also favored higher education for women, a virtually unthinkable concept in that era. Of women he declared that "man has too long degraded them into beasts of burden or into toys to entertain him in his dallying hours." And he added, "We have cut them off from our political privileges." Ritchie even hinted that he might tolerate the idea of women's suffrage.

He was a strong supporter of scientific agriculture, and endorsed the proposal of William Cabell Rives that a chair of agriculture be established at the University of Virginia. Farmers should be educated, he said, in "the rudiments of agricultural chemistry and scientific agriculture." Ritchie urged the formation of local agricultural societies centered in a state organization, and the distribution of prizes and premiums for the discovery of rare products and the operation of model farms. He also advocated the establishment and operation of state-financed agricultural stations.

Ritchie was generous in supporting cultural activities for Richmond. He joined John Marshall and others in a petition to allow James Warrell to establish a museum on the southern edge of Capitol Square, and contributed financially to the project. The museum opened in 1817 but went out of existence in the mid-1830s. Ritchie also bought stock in the Richmond Theatre, which presented the best plays and actors of the day.

The *Enquirer*'s editor was out of sympathy with the prevailing mania for challenging opponents to duels. In contrast to most editors of the time, he seems never to have issued or received a challenge, although he was the recipient of attacks, often from Federalist or Whig sources, that could have moved a man of more conventional principles to summon his critic to the dueling field. The Richmond *Whig* termed him "an impotent dotard and driveller," and the *National Intelligencer* called him "the sovereign dictator of the political opinions of Virginia" and lamented that a great people could be "led about by a weak and wicked editor." The Whigs assailed him as "an artful wirepuller" and "miniature Talleyrand," and spoke of him as "King Ritchie and his prime minister, Dr. Brockenbrough." President Andrew Jackson referred to "the infamous *Enquirer*," and declared that "if such a corrupt press were to approbate my conduct, I should think that in some unguarded moment I had committed some great moral impropriety." By contrast, many admirers called him "Father" Ritchie and "the Napoleon of the Press."

He was frequently attacked as a political boss who ruled Virginia. While he undoubtedly wielded great influence through his newspaper and the Richmond Junto, the term *boss* does not seem appropriate. As Ambler writes in his biography: "He was more frequently opposed to the leading politicians of the state than in accord with them. The methods of the boss were unknown to him. During the twelve years from 1829 to 1841, when he was a power at the Federal court, he recommended only one person for a Federal appointment," and "he scrupulously refrained from any part in the distribution of patronage."

Several efforts were made by party leaders to get Ritchie to come to Washington and establish a party newspaper. Martin Van Buren and Littleton Waller Tazewell sought to persuade him to do this in 1827, so that he might give "the views and opinions of the opposition in Congress." He declined, giving as his reasons "his doubtful qualifications . . . and his attachment to Virginia."

12

In 1844 he was offered the editorship of the Washington *Globe*, the organ of the Republican-Democrats. Once more he declined. But in the following year President James K. Polk invited him to Washington for a personal interview. Polk told him that his services were needed to unite the party, and possibly to save the Union, a cause dear to his heart. Ritchie did not feel that he could refuse. He accordingly resigned from the *Enquirer*, turned it over to his two sons, and moved to the nation's capital. The name of the *Globe* was changed to the *Union*, and he remained as its editor until 1851, when he retired.

The years of his Washington editorship were stormy and highly controversial, with such issues as Texas, Mexico, Oregon, and slavery claiming his and the nation's attention. After relinquishing the editorial chair, he spent much of his remaining three years at Brandon on the James with his daughter Isabella, whose husband, George E. Harrison, owned the historic estate.

Isabella was one of twelve children born to Ritchie and his wife, Isabella Foushee, daughter of Dr. William Foushee, a prominent physician and Richmond's first mayor. Their family life was exemplary, and Ritchie devoted much time and attention to his children, sending them to the best schools. His son William studied in Europe for several years.

Ritchie's editorials were written in a lucid and forceful style that showed the influence of his wide reading. Authors whose works he regarded as especially significant, and whom he was fond of quoting, were Adam Smith, Rousseau, Paine, Malthus, and Voltaire. The attractiveness of his paper was enhanced by the publication of articles by eminent contributors, many of whom signed such pseudonyms as "Cato," "Agricola," "Senex," and "Democritus."

Explaining his decision not to flay his opponents with abusive language, Ritchie stated that "private character is too delicate a subject for any public print. . . . the editor of a public paper who prostitutes it to public abuse or party spirit may be regarded ... as almost as great an enemy to the press as the despot who would wish to paralyze its political influence altogether." He led in promulgating higher standards of ethics for journalists, and proposed a code of rules which served to elevate the tone of the press, although much remained to be done in this respect. Ritchie presided over the first convention of editors held in this country.

In view of the vigor of his editorial pronouncements, it is surprising to read in the words of his biographer that he "rarely made a move of any kind without previously making a diligent effort to ascertain the sentiment of Virginia." While this may well have been his usual procedure, there were glaring exceptions, as when he boldly urged the General Assembly of 1831–32 to abolish slavery.

Thomas Ritchie was a great editor but a wretched businessman. His lack of business acumen kept him financially strapped for most of his married life, and a major reason for his moving to Washington was his hope that he would thereby obtain a higher income and thus remedy his perilous financial condition. His hope was not in vain, for Congress provided him with the funds to cure his fiscal woes.

In the year following his removal to Washington, his son Thomas, Jr., killed John Hampden Pleasants, editor of the rival *Whig*, in a duel. Thomas, Jr., died in 1854, about six weeks before his father's passing—an event that cast a great shadow over the latter's final hours.

Ritchie's two sons, William and Thomas, were not the editors that their father had been. While the *Enquirer* remained influential, and at times it reached a high standard, its quality was never quite as high nor its influence as great as before.

The senior Ritchie was undoubtedly one of this country's foremost editors. His writings were read in all parts of the United States, and he was regarded as the person who most nearly expressed the views of Jefferson and Madison after they passed from the scene. His strong points were a forceful style, sound judgment, sterling integrity, and great industry. His patriotism was intense and his love of Virginia profound.

His funeral in Washington was attended by the president, members of the cabinet, scores of senators and representatives, and members of all parties. Even his onetime enemies came, for they recognized the loftiness of his character and the disinterestedness of his public service. He was buried in Richmond's Hollywood Cemetery.

In 1856, when Representative Preston Brooks of South Carolina caned Charles Sumner of Massachusetts while the latter was seated at his desk in the U.S. Senate, inflicting permanent injuries, the *Enquirer* joined many other Southern papers in approving the caning. "Our approbation... is entire and unreserved," said the *Enquirer*, edited by William F. Ritchie. "It was a proper act, done at the proper time and in the proper manner." Charles Sumner, a leading abolitionist, had been attacking the South and its slaveholders unsparingly, so that the feeling against him throughout the region was intense. Preston Brooks, who attacked him, was the recipient of several gold-headed canes and one gold-handled cowhide from admirers.

In 1857, the year following the caning, O. Jennings Wise, aged twenty-five, returned to Virginia from diplomatic service in Europe, and soon thereafter bought and became editor of the *Enquirer*. In that position he regained for the paper some of the prestige it had lost under the Ritchie brothers. Henry A. Wise, Jennings's father, was governor of Virginia, and Jennings was quick to resent any slurs against the state's chief executive. When Henry Wise was elected governor, Robert Ridgeway, editor of the Richmond *Whig*, wrote that in choosing him the Democrats had abandoned their old-time policy of electing an idiot and had named a lunatic as

15

well. Ridgeway was also wont to refer to Henry Wise as "Old Giz-zard Foot" and "Old Gizzard," since Wise had termed blacks "ebo-shinned and gizzard-footed." All this so infuriated Jennings Wise that he called on Ridgeway at his office and belabored him with a rattan cane. A duel was somehow averted.

Yet Wise fought eight duels in less than two years on the eve of the Civil War. When Patrick Henry Aylett of the *Examiner* was highly critical of Governor Wise in that paper, Jennings de-nounced him in the *Enquirer*. Aylett challenged him to a duel, although Aylett was extremely nearsighted and wore glasses. He missed with his shot, and Wise fired into the air, bowed low, and said, "Sir, I present you to your wife and children."

Although Wise had become highly proficient in Europe as a fencer, he was a wretchedly poor pistol shot, and in his eight duels he seems to have hit only one antagonist. He himself, miracu-lously, was never hit at all. His death at Roanoke Island in 1862 as a captain in the Confederate service cast a pall over Rich-mond.

The *Enquirer*'s prestige remained after his departure. In fact, Douglas S. Freeman says that the *Enquirer* was the most influ-ential paper published in Richmond during the Civil War, al-though he terms John M. Daniel's *Examiner* "much the most in-teresting." Whether the *Enquirer* was, in fact, more influential than the *Examiner* is debatable, but it undoubtedly played an im-portant role. John Mitchel, an Irishman who came to Richmond, was the *Enquirer*'s editor for a part of the hectic war period.

Like all the Richmond newspapers, the *Enquirer* experienced great difficulties when it resumed publication after the conflict was over. Its offices had been destroyed in the conflagration that engulfed the city's business district, as were all the other news-paper offices except those of the *Whig*. The *Enquirer*'s most not-able editor in the postbellum years (it went out of existence in

1877) was James C. Southall, father of James P. C. Southall, the nationally known professor of physics at Columbia University. Southall was editor of the Charlottesville *Chronicle* from 1865 to 1868, in which latter year he joined the *Enquirer*, after also serving in the Underwood Constitutional Convention of 1867–68. Young Southall had been termed by Dr. James Lawrence Cabell of the University of Virginia faculty "by long odds the most finished and promising student that had been educated at the university up to that time" (1846, the year Southall took his M.A. degree at age eighteen).

Southall joined the *Enquirer* when it reversed its stand on the issue of funding, or paying in full, the state debt. The paper had been purchased by the Pennsylvania Central Railroad, and was now in favor of funding, which was in accordance with Southall's views. William Mahone, who represented rival railroad interests, was the funders' major foe. Hot words erupted over this issue between the Richmond *Whig* and the *Enquirer*. The *Whig* asserted that the *Enquirer* was the hired mouthpiece of the Pennsylvania Central Railroad. The latter retorted that the *Whig* was in the pay of the "Virginia Railroad Ring." A duel seemed imminent.

At this point James C. Southall delivered what is believed to have been the first public refusal to fight a duel issued by a prominent Virginian, and one that deserves to be better known. In the columns of his newspaper on March 6, 1872, he wrote:

Mr. Moseley [Alexander Moseley, editor of the *Whig*] doubtless knew, what all know who have been at all conversant with my lifelong opinions, that I would neither give nor accept a challenge to fight a duel, but he no doubt knew as certainly that I am always ready to resist in a proper manner any attack made upon my character or person, and knowing

17

that, he has chosen to defend himself by cowardly recriminations against charges which he knew to be true and declined to resent.

Despite Southall's disclaimer, the authorities arrested him and Moseley, and put them under bond to keep the peace. There was no duel. Southall seems to have been altogether sincere in his determination not to participate in such an encounter, a determination which required great courage in that era. His public statement seems to have had little discernible effect on public opinion, however. It was not until the 1890s, when Joseph Bryan refused a challenge, that a final end was put to this barbarous practice that caused the deaths of so many young men.

When the *Enquirer* ceased publication in 1877, it was the end of the saga of one of Virginia's greatest journals, a saga that had begun nearly three-quarters of a century before and continued through some of the most momentous years in the country's history.

The paper had its ups and downs, but unquestionably its most notable period was when Ritchie was at the editorial helm. "The greatest paper of the Southern states in those years was Thomas Ritchie's Richmond *Enquirer*," Frank Luther Mott writes in his often-quoted history of American journalism. Affectionately known in Richmond as "Tom" Ritchie or "Father" Ritchie, and to a much wider audience as "the Napoleon of the Press," the *Enquirer*'s editor wielded an influence that was national in scope. It is to be doubted if any Virginia editor since his time has been so potent in the nation's councils.

CHAPTER TWO

JOHN HAMPDEN PLEASANTS OF THE *WHIG*

One of the journalistic tragedies of the mid-nineteenth century was the death of John Hampden Pleasants in a duel at age forty-nine. The able and influential editor of the Richmond *Whig* was at the height of his powers when his courageous voice was silenced by the pistol of a rival Richmond editor. As with many invocations of the "code of honor," the confrontation was wholly unnecessary, since the charge leveled at Pleasants was without the slightest foundation. Thomas Ritchie, Jr., of the *Enquirer*, son of the more famous Ritchie, apparently manufactured the allegation in order to provoke Pleasants to a challenge. He called Pleasants "A COWARD," in capital letters, for no reason at all.

The son of Governor James Pleasants, John Hampden Pleasants was born at "Contention" in Goochland County in 1797. He graduated in law from the College of William and Mary in 1817, was admitted to the bar, and began practicing in Lynchburg. But he was bored by the law and decided to enter journalism. He joined the staff of the Lynchburg *Virginian,* a leading paper of that day, and by 1823 was its editor.

The two contending political parties in Virginia were the Republicans (or Democrats) and the Federalists (or Whigs). The *Enquirer* at Richmond spoke eloquently for the former party, but there was no effective journalistic voice at the capital for the latter, even though Richmond was a Whig stronghold. Undismayed by the fierce competition that would be afforded by the well-established *Enquirer,* Pleasants decided to give up his Lynchburg editorship, move to Richmond, and launch the *Whig.* He did so in 1824 with a handpress and a grand total of 275 subscribers.

The twenty-seven-year-old editor was not long in demonstrating his exceptional talents. His style matured steadily, with the result that one commentator, Robert M. Hughes, said that his editorials manifested no less than the "taste of Addison, the repleteness of Burke and the graphic vigor of Macaulay." The same observer declared that "his character was gentle and refined, attracting friend and foe alike." Although Pleasants wielded a trenchant and vigorous pen, he was extremely shy, and was never able to overcome his intense aversion to public speaking.

There was nothing shy about him, however, when he penned his comments on public affairs. He had been in the editorial chair only a few months when the defeat of Ritchie's candidate for the presidency, William H. Crawford, in 1824 led Pleasants to publish a long, tongue-in-cheek commentary under the caption "Death of Thomas Ritchie." The brash young editor of the *Whig* opened with the words "A great man has fallen in Israel! It becomes our painful duty to announce to the public the death of Thomas Ritchie Esq., senior editor of the *Enquirer.*"

In this immensely long editorial, much too long for full quotation, Ritchie is represented in his final hours as exclaiming "O my country!" for he was "firmly impressed with the idea that his personal superintendence was required to hold the sun and stars in their spheres, and make them discharge their diurnal duties to the world which they lighted up." The dying editor was said to be dolefully asking "What will my country—What will the world do without me?"

The *Whig* closed its comments on the passing of Mr. Ritchie as follows:

> For fifteen years he had ruled public opinion in Virginia, and in all that time he had never dissented from the majority. He was so good a Republican that he refused to express any opinion . . . before he had clearly discovered on which side of the question public opinion was. His own sentiments were cheerfully sacrificed to those of the majority. Where is the man, living or dead, who has given stronger devotion than this to the "will of the people" or paid greater respect to the "omnipotence of public opinion"!

It will be recalled that as Charles H. Ambler, Ritchie's biographer, wrote, Ritchie "rarely made a move of any kind without previously making a diligent effort to ascertain the sentiment of Virginia." Thus the *Whig*'s allegation, while stated in hyperbolic terms, was not without foundation.

Pleasants' rivalry with Ritchie was prolonged, but the two men seldom indulged in bitter recriminations against one another. Pleasants termed Ritchie "a dictator," but the latter had heard that charge before from other sources. In a letter to his brother, Ritchie mentioned the allegation as having been made by "that foolish fellow, the editor of the *Whig*," and he added, "I laugh the imputation to scorn." Pleasants also sought to oust his competitor from the lucrative job of public printer, but the latter managed to thwart all such attempts except in 1834, when he lost the post for one year. It was in the presidential campaign of 1840, between William Henry Harrison and Martin Van Buren, that the *Whig* referred to the *Enquirer*'s editor as "an impotent dotard and driveller," as noted in the previous chapter.

While these were sharp words, they were clearly less biting than those which not infrequently passed between rival editors in other cities. Samuel B. Mordecai, in his *Richmond in By-Gone Days,* deplored the manner in which newspapers were so often "disgraced by personalities," and he seemed to regard the Ritchie-Pleasants exchanges as exceeding all proper bounds. "These two papers have been political opponents for many years," he said, "and I would I could add the antagonism had been political only." He felt, amazingly enough, that many newspapers in that era were "unfit for the perusal of a family circle." But Mordecai was notoriously squeamish. He regarded the word "damn" as a level of profanity unworthy of being heard "among gentlemen." Hence his view of the Ritchie-Pleasants relationship was hardly characteristic of his times.

Early in his Richmond career, Pleasants opened the columns of the *Whig* to Isaac Leeser, a twenty-two-year-old Jew who had emigrated from Prussia and settled in Richmond, and who wished to answer an anti-Semitic attack that appeared in the *London Quarterly Review.* Pleasants introduced Leeser's series of articles with the following words:

It is a glorious distinction to our country that here Jews have found a substantial fulfilment of the promise of being restored to the chosen land. That this is his country as much as another's—that the generous and noble spirit of our institutions makes no distinction between Jew and Gentile, Heathen and Mohametan—and if we may quote a quotation so happily and eloquently used recently in the General Assembly, that here "Religion is left free as air, and unbounded as the ocean." Woe to the man who would have it or attempt to make it otherwise!

22

Young Leeser's articles made him a national figure, and in 1829 he accepted a call to the prestigious pulpit of Mikveh Israel in Philadelphia. He is recognized as the founder of the Jewish press in this country and as a pioneer of the Jewish pulpit.

Although Ritchie and Pleasants represented political parties with differing perspectives on important issues, they were in remarkable accord on certain public questions. Both criticized slavery, with Pleasants the more vigorous and consistent critic. Both were strong advocates of a public school system for Virginia and educational opportunities for women, and both favored fairer representation for the western areas of the state. Both men also expressed the highly unorthodox view that an infusion of Northerners would benefit the commonwealth and would tend to arouse Virginians from their lethargy.

Somewhat in contrast to these progressive attitudes, the Whig party was composed mainly of the middle and upper classes, including many slaveowners, and it tended toward conservatism. It leaned toward business and industry and a protective tariff for the benefit of growing western industries such as salt, iron, and wool. Toward the end of the Jeffersonian period the Whigs were not particularly influential. Pleasants' arrival in Richmond was a favorable development for them, and he made the most of it. Within a couple of decades they had elected three governors, and the circulation of the paper had reached 3,000—a large readership for that day and apparently equal to, if not larger than, that of the *Enquirer*.

When the state constitutional convention of 1829–30 met in Richmond, Pleasants joined with Ritchie in advocating fairer representation in the General Assembly for the western portions of Virginia, and a more liberal franchise. Although James Madison, James Monroe, and John Marshall were delegates to the convention, the center of attention was delegate John Randolph of Roanoke, with his eccentric behavior, his extraordinary physical presence, and his brilliant repartee. As a member of the House of Representatives in Washington, Randolph sometimes came on the floor booted and spurred, brandishing a riding crop, with hounds snapping at his heels. In Richmond, by contrast, he appeared throughout the convention dressed in black, with crape on his hat and arm, "in mourning for the old constitution of Virginia," whose demise he feared he was about to witness.

Tall and gaunt, his body reduced to hardly more than skin and bones, with a weatherbeaten face and a falsetto voice, Randolph made no secret of his conservative views. "I am an aristocrat," he proclaimed; "I love liberty, I hate equality." When word was passed that he was about to take the floor, people came running from every direction; and "the house, the lobby and the galleries were crowded almost to suffocation," Hugh Blair Grigsby wrote. Randolph's "Mr. Speaker!" uttered in a melodious treble like the singing of a bird, galvanized the attention of everyone within hearing. Neither he nor Pleasants was pleased with the convention's outcome, though for diametrically opposed reasons. To Randolph, the increased representation for the relatively proletarian West and the extension of the franchise were objectionable. To Pleasants, on the other hand, the concessions made to the West were inadequate.

Pleasants was active in promoting cultural developments. When the Virginia Historical and Philosophical Society (now the Virginia Historical Society) was founded in 1831, he participated in the initial meeting. Some months later, the *Whig* published the minutes of that event, and subsequently gave several columns to an "Address to the Public on the Views of the Society."

In that same year, 1831, Nat Turner's slave insurrection in Southampton County, in the southeastern area of the state near the North Carolina line, terrified the entire South. Pleasants rushed to the scene with Captain Randolph Harrison's troop of light horse, and reported in great detail to his paper concerning

24

the bloody butcheries by slaves of nearly sixty whites, mostly women and children. Pleasants wrote that "it was hardly in the power of rumor itself to exaggerate the atrocities that have been perpetrated by the insurgents: whole families, father, mother, daughters, sons, sucking babes, and school children butchered, thrown into heaps, and left to be devoured by hogs and dogs, or to putrefy on the spot." He added that "at Mr. Levi Waller's his wife and ten children were murdered and piled in one bleeding heap on his floor." The *Whig* editor reassured his readers somewhat by saying that "it is not believed that any outrages were offered to the females."

On his return from the scene, Pleasants wrote a long article in the *Whig*, in the course of which he deplored the blind retaliatory ruthlessness of the whites. "It is with pain we speak of another feature of the Southampton Rebellion," he said,

> for we have been most unwilling to have our sympathies for the sufferers diminished or affected by their misconduct. We allude to the slaughter of many blacks, without trial, and under circumstances of great barbarity. How many have thus been put to death (generally by decapitation or shooting), reports vary; probably, however, some five and twenty and from that to forty; possibly a yet larger number. To the great honor of General Eppes [of Sussex County], he used every precaution in his power to put a stop to the disgraceful procedure.... Another such insurrection will be the signal for the extermination of the whole black population in that quarter of the state where it occurs.

William Lloyd Garrison's inflammatory abolitionist organ, the *Liberator* of Boston, hailed the Southampton massacre, saying: "The first drops of blood, which are but the prelude to a deluge from gathering clouds have fallen.... You have seen, it is to be feared, but the beginning of sorrow.... We have the power to

25

kill *all*—let us therefore continue to apply the whip and forge new fetters!" Such incendiary tirades and the alarm occasioned by the Nat Turner insurrection combined to create an atmosphere in Virginia such as had not been seen since the era of the American Revolution. It suddenly became possible to discuss slavery in all its aspects and to advocate its eventual abolition without suffering dire consequences.

As Virginians confronted the potential violence and horror of slave rebellion, the Turner insurrection was used as an argument in favor of eliminating the Peculiar Institution while there was still time to avoid its consequences. Opposition to slavery was concentrated in the western areas, while its defenders came principally from the Tidewater areas, the Piedmont, and the Southside, where it was a profitable economic venture. The effort to bring slavery to an end, however, came to grief because its foes could propose no practical solution to the problem of what to do with the freed blacks. Few white Virginians could envision permitting the former slaves to remain on the scene in large numbers without the restraints of slavery. Colonization in Africa was considered a practical impossibility, while the white citizens of the Midwest and the still sparsely settled states and territories of the West wanted nothing to do with the relocation of hundreds of thousands of free blacks there.

Pleasants and Ritchie seized upon the situation to urge the elimination of slavery over a period of time, with Pleasants the more vehement and outspoken of the two. His *Whig* advocated the use of federal funds toward the desired end and opposed the expulsion of free Negroes to Africa, whereas the *Enquirer* opposed the former and endorsed the latter. On the subject of forcing free blacks to leave the country of their nativity, the *Whig* declared that this would be "unequivocal, unalloyed and unqualified tyranny . . . the most lawless, violent and despotic means ever attempted in the United States." The paper expressed hatred of the

Northern abolitionists, however, and asserted that if their fellow citizens did not "go about hanging these fanatical wretches," Southerners should cut off trade with the North. At the same time, Pleasants was unsparing in his criticism of chattel servitude, saying that the system was doomed. "The moment statesmen were permitted to examine the moral foundation and the pernicious effect of slavery," he wrote, "and the press was unshackled to proclaim their sentiments and to combat in the cause of reason, justice and the common good, that moment the decree of abolition was registered in the book of fate. It must be so; it cannot be otherwise."

Pleasants' outspokenness was not approved by everyone. Newspapers advocating emancipation of the blacks should be suppressed, a person signing himself "Appomattox" declared. Pleasants believed that "Appomattox" was Benjamin Watkins Leigh. Whatever his identity, both the *Whig* and the *Enquirer* assailed him. On the other hand, citizens held meetings of indignation at which both papers were denounced and withdrawal of subscriptions was threatened.

All the agitation at the session of 1831–32 for drastic action to get rid of the slave system came to nothing, and a reaction in the opposite direction set in. From that time forward, defense of slavery was the watchword, and the two Richmond papers became less militant, although from time to time the *Whig* continued its attacks on aspects of the Peculiar Institution.

That paper also became infuriated during the session of 1835–36 when the state legislature passed what the historian Clement Eaton has called "the most intolerant law" ever placed on that body's statute books. The legislation was "far worse than lynching and lynch's law, and a reflection on the state that such deformed crudities are submitted in the shape of bills," the *Whig* roared. The paper went on to declare that "the country has never been so sick of any legislature, or with such good reason...."

about forty of its members were the most stupid legislators we have ever seen here."

The legislation which so aroused the *Whig*'s ire provided that anyone circulating or printing a book, pamphlet, or newspaper for the purpose of persuading slaves to rebel, or denying the right of masters to property in their slaves, was guilty of a felony. It also stipulated severe punishment for any member of an abolition society who entered the state to contend that "the owners of slaves have no property in the same, or advocate or advise the abolition of slavery."

Pleasants' low opinion of the Virginia General Assembly was shared by John Warden, a prominent Richmond lawyer. Warden told all and sundry that he didn't think the legislators had "sense enough to carry guts to a bear." This uncomplimentary deliverance so incensed the solons that they had the sergeant-at-arms arrest Warden and bring him before them. He was ordered to get on his knees and apologize. This he did, but in the following elliptical terms: "Mr. Speaker, I did say that your honors were not fit to carry guts to a bear. I now retract that assertion, and acknowledge that you are fit."

Warden's physiognomy was such as had seldom been seen. "His mouth was enormous, but his tongue was too large for his mouth," according to one observer, which led a wag to compose the following:

> Reader, tread lightly o'er his sod,
> For if he gapes, you are gone, by God!

Pleasants was much less deliberate and careful in composing his editorials than was Ritchie, Colonel John A. Parker wrote in the Norfolk *Landmark* under the pseudonym "Essex." "Ritchie never prepared or published an editorial without bestowing on it thought and deliberation, and with it added tact, judgment and prudence," Parker said.

Pleasants, on the other hand, never stopped to deliberate, and took no stock in policy or prudence. He was bold, daring and aggressive . . . one of the finest paragraphists I have ever known—racy and sprightly. He would often be seen walking the streets of Richmond, suddenly drop into any store, and there dash off one of his most brilliant editorials, send it to the *Whig* office, and seem to forget what he had done. . . .

Mr. Pleasants never resorted to personalities. . . . When he made attacks they were open and manly; his blows were felt; he was ever ready to acknowledge and make amends of any injustice committed. He had many noble and generous traits of character.

Colonel Parker explained that he held this high opinion of Pleasants even though he was opposed to his political principles.

The "Log Cabin and Hard Cider" presidential campaign of 1840 came close to attaining a new high, or low, in the bamboozlement of the public. It was the first presidential election in which the expanded Jacksonian electorate was openly wooed by the politicos. Incredible hokum was indulged in by both sides. William Henry Harrison, born to luxury in a Virginia mansion and living on a handsome Ohio estate—miraculously transformed into a "log cabin" for the campaign—was contending with Martin Van Buren. The latter was charged by the opposition with lolling luxuriously in the White House, eating with gold spoons from silver plate, and perfuming his whiskers with French eau de cologne, while riding about in a gilded coach imported from Great Britain. Seventeen log cabins were placed at strategic points around Virginia, "adorned with large numbers of coonskins, gourds, and cider barrels." A live bear and three stuffed bearskins were on view at all Virginia meetings for Harrison. When Daniel Webster came to Richmond in behalf of the Harrison candidacy, "log cabins surmounted by live raccoons, and canoes filled with white boys dressed as Indians, were transported through the leading streets on carts."

Editors in that era were ready and willing to go to absurd lengths in behalf of their party's candidate, and Pleasants was no exception. He depicted Harrison as one of the great Indian fighters of all time, an immortal hero, while attacking Van Buren in a manner that, in modern times, would almost have embarrassed a Tammany ward heeler.

When returns from the election began trickling in, it appeared that the outcome might turn on Virginia's vote. The *Whig* immediately began ridiculing the pro-Van Buren "Suabian Dutch" in the Shenandoah Valley for their stupidity. The paper announced its unwillingness to accept the results of a national election which turned on "300 spurious Dutch votes," and a vigilance committee was formed apparently to reject and repudiate the outcome if Van Buren carried the state by a narrow margin. As if this were not a sufficiently drastic procedure, some Whigs supposedly planned to spring a coup d'état "by which Van Buren was to have been seized on the eve of his second inaugural and carried to the mountains of North Carolina." Ritchie's biographer, Charles H. Ambler, says "later evidence showed" that such a plan had actually been drawn up. "Although Pleasants later denied the existence of any such revolutionary plot, explaining it all as a hoax upon Father Ritchie, it cannot be denied that the Whigs regarded their predicament as serious and that they contemplated a resort to force," Ambler writes. Van Buren was not elected, but the fact—if it is a fact—that such a scheme was even contemplated is a commentary on the hectic politics of the era.

Other and less partisan matters also elicited Pleasants' editorial attention. The relatively primitive medicine of the mid-nineteenth century was almost helpless in combatting epidemics of cholera, smallpox, and yellow fever. Nobody knew what caused them. The Richmond *Whig*'s prescription for coping with cholera was to urge that the city council prohibit the bringing of watermelons, cabbages, and cucumbers to market. This kind of reasoning was no more far-fetched than the medical profession's advice at another time that the way to thwart cholera was: "Wear a flannel shirt or jacket, flannel drawers and yarn stockings. . . . never permit any fruit at all to be in your house, or any vegetable except rice and well-cooked potatoes."

The *Whig*, along with the *Enquirer*, strongly urged the establishment of a statewide system of public schools in the 1840s. This movement gained momentum, and conventions were held at various points in Virginia in the hope of arousing public opinion. "That legislature would achieve immortal honor," said the *Whig*, "which would boldly mortgage the revenue of the state for fifty years to come, if nothing less would do it, for the education of the children of the commonwealth." But opposition to the use of taxation for the purpose of establishing a system of public schools led to the proposal's defeat, despite strenuous efforts in its behalf. In the antebellum era Virginia was largely dependent upon hundreds of small, privately supported academies, where the classical emphasis was pronounced and whose pupils came from well-circumstanced families. Latin, Greek, and mathematics were emphasized, and the pedagogical facilities were often ludicrously inadequate. Instruction was frequently offered in log cabins, with little or no equipment. One of the most famous of these schools was Concord Academy, operated in Caroline County by Frederick W. Coleman. Living accommodations were decidedly Spartan, and instructional equipment virtually nonexistent. Moreover, "boys were knocked up at all hours of the night and summoned to the recitation room," said W. Gordon McCabe, himself a famous schoolmaster after the war. "Sophocles with your candles, young gentlemen" was the frequent admonition, and the sleepy youngsters had to rouse themselves and give their best translation of the works of the Greek tragedian. Yet this incredibly unstructured curriculum sometimes produced excellent results.

As controversy mounted over slavery, there was much criticism of the free blacks in Virginia and the other Southern states. Many white Virginians seemed to feel that they were a menace and more likely to cause serious trouble than the slaves. The *Whig*, on the other hand, pronounced the low-grade white a "far greater pest" than the free black. When Governor William ("Extra Billy") Smith repeatedly urged that the more than 50,000 free Negroes be expelled from the state, the *Whig* said, shortly after the governor went out of office, that many free Negroes "in all relations of life" are "as respectful and good citizens as . . . the ex-governor himself."

At the same time, the *Whig* shared the alarm of most Virginians over the incendiary attacks of the Northern abolitionists, and of an abolitionist nearer home—Cassius M. Clay of Kentucky, who was accused of trying to incite a slave insurrection. Clay was publishing at Lexington a journal called the *True American,* and its exhortations became so inflammatory that it was suppressed in 1845 and its presses shipped out of town. Pleasants commented in the *Whig*, "We feel no sympathy for Mr. Clay, a member of that family of fanatics who, pernicious ever to society and its peace, are more especially pernicious to the cause which they undertook to promote."

Pleasants was instrumental in preventing a duel between William S. Archer, U.S. senator from Virginia, and William F. Ritchie. Archer made a personal attack on Ritchie's father on a Richmond street because of something published in the *Enquirer.* Young Ritchie heard about it and, without consulting his father, sought out Archer and slapped his face. This led to the inevitable challenge. Pleasants got word of it and immediately began efforts to prevent the encounter. He had great influence with Archer, and argued with him that William Ritchie had merely performed an act of duty in slapping Archer's jaws—and that if Ritchie fell at his hands, it would be regarded as murder in all civilized countries. Archer withdrew the challenge.

Young William Ritchie was nearly blind, and even with glasses could barely distinguish objects. Yet he risked another duel in 1843, and with Pleasants, despite the friendly act the latter had performed for him not long before. This quarrel concerned some words in the *Whig*. A duel was prevented by the intervention of Ritchie's father and two other prominent citizens, James Lyons and J. W. Pegram.

Bad blood between Pleasants and the Ritchie brothers, Thomas, Jr., and William F., continued after the senior Ritchie moved to Washington in 1845. The younger Ritchies appeared to be deeply hostile to the *Whig* editor. Despite Pleasants' frequently expressed strong aversion to Northern abolitionists, a communication appeared in the *Enquirer* in 1846 over the signature "Macon," charging that Pleasants was planning to establish an abolitionist journal. On its face the allegation was absurd, and Pleasants denounced it at once as a falsehood. "Macon," who was actually Thomas Ritchie, Jr., then came forth with the equally ridiculous charge that Pleasants was "A COWARD."

The editor of the *Whig* abhorred dueling, but in the prevailing climate of opinion, he felt that there was nothing for him to do but challenge Ritchie. This was evidently what Ritchie—described as an "experienced and enthusiastic duellist"—wanted.

The challenge issued by the inexperienced Pleasants was not in accordance with protocol prescribed by the code duello. He advised Ritchie that he would appear at dawn next day on the south side of the James, just upstream from the Manchester cotton factory, armed with pistols and prepared to shoot him on sight.

Ritchie protested, in a letter now on file at the Virginia Historical Society, that the challenge was "not in the form which is justified by men of honor," since "it gives the challenging party the privilege of selecting the time, place and weapons, a right which, according to all usage, belongs to the challenged." Furthermore, said Ritchie, "both time and place are so selected as to occasion great inconvenience and danger to all parties concerned from legal prosecution." He concluded by pronouncing the terms "savage, sanguinary and revolting," but said he would accept them, nevertheless.

Pleasants arrived at the appointed spot armed not only with a revolver in his coat pocket and a pistol in each hand, but also with a bowie knife in his vest and a sword cane under his left arm. Ritchie, likewise a walking arsenal, had two pistols stuck in his belt, a revolver in his coat pocket, a cutlass in his belt, and a pistol in each hand. As events later showed, Pleasants had no intention of using this vast array of firepower and cutlery, whereas Ritchie evidently was bent on seriously wounding or killing his opponent.

This unorthodox confrontation on the field of honor began with the antagonists standing some two hundred yards apart. Pleasants began walking slowly toward Ritchie, and neither fired until they were within about thirty yards. Ritchie then began shooting directly at Pleasants, whereas the latter wasted his only shot in the air. Ritchie scored several hits as Pleasants staggered toward him. Collapsing and bleeding profusely from several wounds, Pleasants made a pass at Ritchie with his sword cane, inflicting a superficial facial cut. He fell and was carried from the field.

Pleasants lived for two days. On his death bed he said he had taken the ball out of his pistol the night before, since "I didn't want to kill him; I went there to show him that I was not a coward." He expressed pleasure that Ritchie was not hurt, called him "a brave fellow," and urged that he not be blamed in any way.

The death of John Hampden Pleasants at the height of his career, in a completely unnecessary duel, was a sad blow to Richmond and Virginia. Members of all political parties attended his funeral and his burial in Hollywood Cemetery, and there was profound sorrow over his passing. Young Dr. Moses D. Hoge, a close friend of Pleasants and later the most eminent clergyman in Richmond, made the following comment:

> Honor is appeased: put that in one scale; and one of the most brilliant lights of Virginia has been quenched ... and his slayer by this act has fastened the undying worm to his own heart, several families have been filled with bitter, hopeless lamentation, and a whole community has been made to mourn: put that in the other.

When Ritchie was tried for the murder of Pleasants, there was a lengthy hearing. But when the case went to the jury, that body, without leaving the box, rendered a verdict of "not guilty." This was received with loud applause in the courtroom—evidence of the virtual impossibility, in that age, of convicting anyone for killing his adversary in a duel, even when the victim was as greatly admired as Pleasants.

On the slain editor's tomb in Hollywood is the following:

> A Republican Whig editor from principle,
> of unquestioned ability and patriotism,
> of self-sacrificing, gallant and generous
> bearing, the unyielding advocate of the
> great principles of the Constitution, as
> understood and practiced by its founders, with
> A genius above talent
> A courage above heroism
> This monument is erected to the memory of
> their distinguished editor by his surviving brother Whigs.

Thomas Ritchie, Jr., lived only two years after his fateful encounter with John Hampden Pleasants. Some said he died of re-

35

morse. Since he left $25,000 in his will to Pleasants' daughter, this seems entirely possible. It appears obvious that he wished to make amends for causing the death of the most courageous foe of slavery in Virginia, and one of the nineteenth century's authentic editorial geniuses.

Following Pleasants' death, Oliver P. Baldwin, formerly of the Richmond *Republican,* assisted briefly in the *Whig*'s editorial department until Richard H. Toler took over the editorship. After Toler's death in 1848, Alexander Moseley was in editorial charge for a few years.

During that time a bitter newspaper controversy erupted over the plan to establish Hollywood cemetery. The *Whig* had favored the plan, but when the rival *Enquirer* also waxed enthusiastic and Thomas H. Ellis, a leading Democrat, became president of the Hollywood Cemetery Company, the *Whig* reversed its position and began making vicious attacks on the entire scheme. It echoed the theory advanced by the *Times* of London that volatile gases from decaying bodies endangered the health of persons in the area. The paper argued repeatedly that the proximity of the city waterworks to the proposed burial ground would be extremely hazardous. "If people, every time they take a glass of water, a cup of tea or coffee, imagine they are swallowing the remains of a defunct enemy or friend," the paper argued, "would that not be sufficient reason against the incorporation of this burying ground?" Hollywood's advocates prevailed, however, despite the *Whig*'s campaign, and the cemetery was opened.

After Moseley's retirement as editor of the *Whig*, editorial direction of the paper was in the hands of James E. Heath, who had served nearly two decades before as, in effect, the first editor of the *Southern Literary Messenger.* Under Heath, the *Whig* abandoned its crusade against Hollywood. The enterprise prospered. Soon after Heath relinquished the editorial reins, Robert Ridgeway took over. His attacks on Governor Henry A. Wise as a "lunatic" and "idiot" aroused the ire of Wise's son, O. Jennings Wise, who administered a caning to Ridgeway in his office, as already noted. On the approach of the Civil War, Ridgeway expressed such strong opposition to secession that he was forced out as editor in 1861. Alexander Moseley succeeded him and was in editorial charge until the last year of the war.

At the close of hostilities, the *Whig* was the only Richmond newspaper whose offices were not destroyed in the conflagration that virtually wiped out the city's business district. It reappeared at once, on April 8, 1865, as a Union paper, according to an announcement in that issue. This state of things did not continue indefinitely, however. Alexander Moseley returned as editor in 1868.

The subsequent career of the *Whig*, which under Colonel William C. Elam became an organ of William Mahone's Readjusters, will be noted in the pages to come.

CHAPTER THREE

JOHN MONCURE DANIEL OF THE
EXAMINER

The most brilliantly slashing writer of newspaper editorials in Virginia in the nineteenth century was John Moncure Daniel of the Richmond *Examiner*. His editorial style was both eminently readable and notably more vituperative than that of any of his contemporaries, if that is conceivable.

When the War between the States began, Daniel swiftly informed his readers that Yankees were "vain," "arrogant," "infernal scoundrels" and "incarnate demons," and that cowardice was "carefully inculcated" in them "from birth." President Lincoln was "a baboon," "a common sot," "the Yahoo President," whose road to the White House was "strewn with condensed lumps of imbecility, buffoonery and vulgar malignity." Kentucky-born Major Robert Anderson, U.S. Army, commander of Fort Sumter at the time of the bombardment that began the war, was a "toad-spotted traitor to his section."

Daniel was born in Stafford County in 1825, the son of a country doctor who was chiefly responsible for his early schooling. At age fifteen he moved to Richmond to live with his father's uncle, Judge Peter V. Daniel. A few years later, like several other subjects of this volume, young Daniel embarked briefly on a legal career, only to find it not to his liking. He became librarian of the Patrick Henry Society, a group of young men interested in reading and debating. Shortly thereafter he was made editor of the *Southern Planter,* and in 1847 he became editor of the newly established Richmond *Examiner.* In the latter post, which he occupied for the rest of his relatively short life, he combined a superb journalistic instinct with a business acumen that made the paper highly profitable. Yet Daniel was primarily concerned with his paper's editorial side, and he did not hesitate to throw out lucrative advertisements to make way for editorial matter.

When he took over the editorial reins of the *Examiner* in 1847 at the age of twenty-two, Daniel set out to make himself widely known and as widely hated by deliberately attacking almost every prominent man in Virginia. Many of these individuals detested him for the rest of their lives. Daniel was extremely unpopular, but seemed oblivious of or indifferent to the fact, so long as he was read. And he certainly was.

With his genius for making enemies, it was inevitable that Daniel would be involved in duels, a hazard he accepted willingly. He and Edgar Allan Poe, who was as temperamental as he, got into an altercation when Poe visited Richmond in 1848. The poet had had negotiations with the editor about contributions to the *Examiner*, and there was friction of one sort or another. Finally Poe became so exasperated that he sent a challenge to Daniel. The "latter preferred to settle the matter alone in the *Examiner* office," J. H. Whitty, an authority on Poe, wrote in the Richmond *Evening Journal* on January 19, 1909. The poet, it seems, was in his cups when he went to the newspaper, and "was hardly in any condition to fight a duel." And Whitty's account goes on:

> When he entered, Daniel was sitting near a table on which were displayed two very large pistols.... Daniel, in a cool and quiet manner, asked Poe to be seated.... Instead of the usual formalities of the code, he suggested that they settle the dispute then and there.... he pointed to the pistols, ready for use.... Poe began to sober up. He asked some questions about their difficulty, and soon became convinced that matters had been exaggerated.

At about that time friends came in and all differences were smoothed out. There was no duel. A more than adequate literary commentator, Daniel wrote an article on Poe's literary significance that the French poet Charles Baudelaire incorporated liberally and without credit in his often-quoted and influential essay on Poe. Only in recent years was it made evident that Baudelaire's impressive insights into Poe's ultimate significance were in reality Daniel's.

Another example of Poe's erratic behavior during that visit to Richmond in 1848 is related in the papers of the sculptor Edward V. Valentine. Dr. George Rawlings, a local physician, was making a professional call in the building where Poe's friend Hugh Pleasants resided. Rawlings came up unannounced, and found "the author of 'The Raven' standing pistol in hand on the second landing of the stair, and apparently about to fire at the keyhole. Needless to say, the worthy doctor departed without standing on the order of his going." Whether Poe pulled the trigger is not known.

The preposterous irrationality of devotees of the code duello is nowhere better illustrated than in the circumstances surrounding a duel fought by Daniel in 1852, apparently his first. He and

Edward C. Johnston of the *Whig* got into a discussion of the artistic merits of Powers' statue, the *Greek Slave*. They differed strongly in their views, and in an incredible fit of fatuity decided that the way to settle the matter was on "the field of honor." They exchanged shots, but fortunately both missed.

An early example of Daniel's "damn everything" style is seen in his comments on the ceremonies attending the laying of the cornerstone for Thomas Crawford's equestrian statue of George Washington in Capitol Square in 1850. The *Examiner* was revolted by the "essential stupidity" of the entire proceeding. The conveyance in which the principal dignitaries rode was "a vulgar, open carriage, fit only for a snob or parvenue." The Masons, in laying the cornerstone, "went through their mummeries—winding up the same with a most doleful and lonesome psalm tune." And "several brass bands performed with unexampled fury in alarming propinquity to one another," while "the Sons of Temperance, remarkable for their red noses and faces, made their appearance . . . in great force."

When substantial numbers of farmers from the North settled in Virginia in the 1840s and 1850s, bringing with them scientific farming methods and free labor, their coming was hailed by the Richmond *Whig* and *Enquirer,* but the *Examiner* was choleric in its comments. It opposed this "vandal invasion of Virginia," with its "fragrant hordes of adventurers fresh from the . . . codfisheries of the Bay State," who would convert areas of the commonwealth into "a paradise of onions, squashes, string beans and 'liberty.' "

As for Daniel's appearance, his coworker Robert W. Hughes said that his features were "patrician and classical," while his "raven black hair was worn long." And Hughes went on to say:

His well-shapen nose was exceptionally but pleasantly prominent. His mouth was large with well-developed, and a lady would say, bewitchingly expressive lips. His dark brown eyes

were brilliant and piercing: his complexion sombre, his vis-
age thin: and his handsome classical countenance capable of
expressing the most winning kindliness, or the most repel-
lent scorn. . . . His feeble physique was rendered more fragile
by a painful and racking nervousness, which often over-
threw his self-control, and subjected his naturally clear, just
mind to . . . an irascible temper.

While surviving photographs show him cleanshaven, during the
war he had a heavy black mustache and black beard.

A lifelong bachelor, Daniel said that he didn't want to marry,
but that if he did, "it must be with the explicit understanding
that he and his wife should occupy separate houses." He added
that "there are but two ways to manage a woman—to club her or
to freeze her."

In 1853 Daniel was appointed chargé d'affaires at the court of
Turin, or Sardinia. He sold the *Examiner*, reserving the right to
repurchase it. After three years in Italy he was elevated to the
rank of minister. The promotion came despite an uproar created
throughout Europe by a letter he wrote to a friend in Richmond a
few months after his arrival, caustically criticizing not only Italy,
its customs and manners, but Europe and Europeans in general.
His letter, marked "Strictly Private and Confidential," somehow
got into the *Examiner*, and then was translated and republished
throughout Italy and various other countries. Among Daniel's observations were these: "The meanness, the filthy life, the stupid-
ities of all the countries that I have seen, surpass all I expected.
. . . Courts in Turin stink of garlic, as does the whole country. . . .
I receive visits from diplomats with hands as empty as their
hearts, and find the whole concern more trashy than I had ever
imagined."

The stir caused by such animadversions can well be surmised, and Daniel offered his resignation, only to have it rejected by the State Department. The episode, needless to say, cast a shadow over his entire diplomatic assignment. His views on European ways did not, however, discourage the noted Italian patriot, Garibaldi, a native of Nice, in France, who called on Daniel and asked him to get the United States to annex Nice, since he and his fellow citizens there "loathed the French."

Daniel resigned his ministerial post in 1860, as war clouds gathered in America, and returned to Richmond early in 1861. Surprisingly, when he arrived on these shores, he was not in favor of secession according to Robert W. Hughes, who had had charge of the *Examiner* during his absence and who had served under him before his departure for Turin. Daniel thought the Deep South was wrong in withdrawing from the Union. However, since it had now done so, he believed that Virginia and the rest of the region should do likewise in order that a united slave-state front might be presented.

Once he had made up his mind, no one was more vitriolic in denouncing all who disagreed with him. They were "old fogies" and "conceited old ghosts who crawled from a hundred damp graves to manacle their state, and to deliver her up as a handmaid to the hideous chimpanzee from Illinois." Richmond's two delegates to the peace conference in Washington designed to head off the looming catastrophe were "consummate traitors." Furthermore, anybody who thought Northern men were as brave as Southern men simply needed his head examined, since the Northerners' "foremost and most admired" had been "kicked, caned and cowhided as unresistingly as Spaniel dogs."

When the guns boomed at Sumter, Daniel was unbelievably optimistic as to the outcome of the war. He had utter contempt for the Yankees, of course; in addition to being cowardly they were "abominable villains," "thieves upon principle, assassins at heart." "The Yankee," he said, "is a toady because he can no more refrain from bootlicking than a cat can keep its paws off a mouse."

Also, according to the editor of the *Examiner*, the North was facing bankruptcy for lack of Southern products and trade, and the people there would have to migrate to the West or starve. He saw New York City as on the way down the drain: "In the silent streets, the deserted hotels, the closed places of amusement and recreation, every place and everything witnesses that the glory of the once-proud metropolis is gone, gone too, forever, for the trade of the South will never return."

Except for two limited periods, Daniel's vast bellicosity toward the North was not translated into membership in the Confederate fighting forces, for he was wholly unfitted for military service. His health was delicate, and his physique frail; of medium height, he never weighed more than 120 pounds. Anxious to serve, however, he did so as a major in 1861 and then again in 1862, receiving "an honorable wound" in the Seven Days battles. The elaborate and almost unprecedented equipment with which he had gone into battle included a tent of his own design, a complete cooking apparatus, a valet, and a cook. Stonewall Jackson's orderly said Daniel's military accoutrements approached the foppish. The wound in Daniel's right arm was not severely disabling, and he returned to his editorial desk.

In complete contrast to his later unremitting assaults on Jefferson Davis, Daniel hailed the President of the Confederate States with enthusiasm upon his inauguration at Montgomery in 1861. He urged Davis to move his government to Richmond, saying his presence there "would be worth 50,000 men." When Davis made the move early in 1862, Daniel demanded a dictatorship with Davis in control. "To the dogs with constitutional questions and moderation," the *Examiner* proclaimed. "What we need is an effective resistance."

At about this time, Colonel Marmaduke Johnson of Richmond was so infuriated by reflections on his patriotism and integrity in the *Examiner* that when he saw Daniel approaching on Franklin Street in broad daylight, he began shooting. Daniel unlimbered his own shooting iron and fired back. Both men missed, and the police arrived and arrested them. They were placed under bond to keep the peace.

This fracas grew out of an editorial in which the paper ridiculed various prominent Virginians who temporarily favored the Union in the convention that was considering secession in early 1861. There were references to "the Jackass from Petersburg, the Hyena from Monongalia, the curly-headed poodle from Richmond." Colonel Marmaduke Johnson was "the sleek fat pony from Richmond, who neighed submission: one master for him would be as good as another; what he went in for was good feeding, and he believed he could get that from Old Abe as well as anybody else."

John Letcher, Virginia's governor, also incurred the savage wrath of Editor Daniel, apparently because he tried to prevent secession in early 1861. "By some inscrutable dispensation of Providence," said the *Examiner*, Governor Letcher "has been inflicted as a curse upon the people of Virginia." The paper went on to say that "the evils and ravages of the war have been borne by those who saw their homes made desolate by the neglect and improvidence of an imbecile governor . . . one who never had a single patriotic instinct." Letcher, however, did not summon Daniel to "pistols at ten paces," as he might well have done; or, as a Richmond columnist indicated forty years later, he might have used more unconventional means. As this scribe wrote: "It does honor to humanity to think that some of his [Daniel's] victims had sufficient self-control to challenge him to the field of honor instead of going after him with a meat cleaver."

Less than two months after the South's victory at First Manassas, an invasion of the North was demanded by the *Examiner*, which declared that the South could have 500,000 men in readiness for the operation. "Ohio and Pennsylvania ought to feel the terrors which agitate the cowardly and the guilty, when retributive vengeance is at hand," the paper bellowed. Where the Southern commanders were to find half a million properly equipped soldiers for such an expedition was not explained.

General Robert E. Lee was the butt of invidious comments from the *Examiner*, as well as other papers, early in the war. Lee had trained most of the forces that overcame the Union army at First Manassas and had had an important role in devising the successful strategy there, although he was not present on the field, as President Davis kept him in Richmond. Davis then sent him on a vaguely defined and virtually impossible military mission in the West Virginia mountains. It was not a success, and on his return to Richmond he was sneered at in the press as "Evacuating" Lee and "Granny" Lee. When President Davis then dispatched him to Charleston and Savannah for the uninspiring task of fortifying those ports and adjacent waterways, the *Examiner* expressed the hope that Lee would prove more effective with the spade than he had been with the sword. Lee remarked sardonically that it was "too bad that all our worst generals are in command of the armies and our best generals are editing the newspapers."

The South was disheartened by the serious reverses at Fort Henry and Fort Donelson on the Tennessee River, and at Roanoke Island in North Carolina. Judah P. Benjamin, the Jewish secretary of war, was much criticized for the Roanoke Island disaster and was shifted to secretary of state. Daniel commented sourly, "The representation of the synagogue remains full."

As McClellan's Union army moved along the Peninsula toward Richmond in the spring of 1862, Daniel lamented that "Confederate generals never attack anybody." The women, this hard-shelled bachelor surprisingly asserted, were the only ones who were supporting the Confederacy to the limit of their abilities.

While Lee strained every nerve to build defenses for the city, the *Examiner* contrasted Stonewall Jackson's fighting qualities in the Shenandoah Valley campaign with Lee's ditch digging. Another paper dubbed him the "King of Spades."

With the wounding of General Joseph E. Johnston at the Battle of Seven Pines, General Lee took command. The *Examiner* was as sarcastic as ever, remarking, "Evacuating Lee, who has never yet risked a single battle with the invader, is commanding general." These journalistic sneers did much to undermine Lee's temporary standing with the public. When, however, a few weeks later McClellan was driven from the city's gates, "Marse Robert" became the idol of the South.

The editor of the *Examiner* was deeply disturbed over the amount of drunkenness in the streets of wartime Richmond, with soldiers back from the front as the guilty parties. The paper lamented:

One cannot go amiss for whiskey in Richmond. The curse and filth of it reek along the streets. It is eating into the vitals of society. It is killing our soldiers, making brutes of our officers, "stealing the brains of our generals," taxing our army with endless court-martials, and *sinking our great struggle into a pandemonium of revelry, recklessness and mad license.* Scarcely a night passes in Richmond but the sound of drunken riot may be heard on the streets, as the revelers pass from brothel to brothel, or reel along the streets seeking for shelter and home.

If this seems an extreme picture, consider the comments of the *Enquirer* a bit later. It declared that "upwards of a dozen drunken soldiers were knocked down in the streets and robbed Saturday night." On another occasion it said: "One has to go into the streets of the city [at night] and see hundreds of good looking

young men wearing the uniform of their country's service em-
bruted by liquor, converted into barroom vagabonds."

The *Examiner* also criticized the "gamblers of Richmond" who
had "multiplied as the lice of Egypt." The paper noted that "a vir-
tuous deacon" had been captured in a gambling saloon, and on
the same occasion "it is said that a cabinet minister, who was in
one of those inner chambers reserved for distinguished guests
and sacred to the mysteries of 'blue checks,' effected his escape
by jumping from a window."

The historian Bell I. Wiley termed Richmond "the true mecca
of prostitutes." Mayor Mayo found it impossible to close all the
houses of ill fame, and the *Examiner* commented: "If the mayor
lacks any incentive to stimulate . . . breaking up the resorts of ill
fame, let him visit military hospitals and look upon the human
forms lying there, wrecked upon the treacherous shoals of vice
and passion which encounter the soldier at the corner of every
street, lane and alley of the city." The paper called Richmond "a
bloated metropolis of vice."

Examiner editorials "were read at the head of regiments, and
copies of it were as eagerly sought by the men in the trenches as
their rations," Robert W. Hughes declared. It is surprising,
therefore, that John Hampden Chamberlayne, a lieutenant doing
frequent staff work for General A. P. Hill and later editor of the
Richmond *State,* wrote in 1862 to George W. Bagby: "Tell me
something of John Daniel. I see his paper sometimes, it lacks
force mightily. Is his circulation waning, that he should feel the
ground falling under him?" If anybody else ever accused Daniel
of lacking force, it is not of record.

Daniel was his vigorous and derisive self in criticism of the
conduct of Generals J. E. B. Stuart and Wade Hampton on their
incursion into Pennsylvania when they raided Chambersburg.
The *Examiner* denounced the "pretty civilities showered by
Stuart and Hampton on the Dutch farmers of Pennsylvania dur-

ing their raid on Chambersburg.... Again and again have
Southern people had occasion to know the ridiculous figure they
make, the contempt they bring upon themselves, and the positive
injury they invite by their sentimental tenderness for Yankees,
and their monkey chivalry.... Chivalry is a very noble quality.
But we do not get our idea of it from the mincings of dandy preachers and parlor geldings."

When the "bread riot" broke out in Richmond in the spring of
1863 the other papers cooperated with the Confederate authorities by not mentioning it, but the *Examiner*, which had become
bitterly critical of President Davis, refused his request for silence. On the contrary, Daniel's organ gave the event extensive
coverage, and denounced the local and Confederate authorities
for not shooting the looters. Furthermore, said the *Examiner*, the
mob which stole foodstuffs and other articles after smashing
store windows was composed of "a handful of prostitutes, professional thieves, Irish and Yankee hags, gallows-birds from all
lands but our own." This picturesque description of the rioters
bore only a remote relation to the facts.

In their constant, snarling criticisms of President and Mrs.
Davis, Daniel and his associate editor, Edward A. Pollard, were
completely unfair. The president of the Confederacy, they said, sat
"serene upon the frigid heights of an infallible egotism...
wrapped in sublime self-complacency, turning a deaf ear to all."
Also: "Every military misfortune of the country is palpably and
confessedly due to the personal interference of Mr. Davis." And a
government ought to head a nation, not be "its tail, its posterior."
As for Mrs. Davis, if she entertained, she was not being sufficiently self-sacrificing for the cause; if she didn't entertain, she
was being stingy. The *Whig* was also extremely critical.

With escalating inflation causing a sharp rise in the cost of
everything, the Confederate House passed a joint resolution in
1864 providing additional compensation for Davis to cover "lights

and fuel for the presidential mansion" as well as forage for four horses. The *Examiner* had its usual tantrum, saying that the proposal violated the Confederate constitution, which stipulated that the president's compensation "shall neither be increased nor diminished" during his term. If he can't live on his salary, "let him resign," the paper declared.

R. G. H. Kean, head of the Bureau of War for the Confederate government, wrote in his diary of the harm done to the Southern cause by the unremitting newspaper criticism, and he added: "What the *Examiner* and the *Whig* propose to themselves as to the good to be produced by stirring up opposition, distrust and hatred toward the president, I cannot imagine." It seems quite probable that these unfair attacks did much to undermine confidence in the Davis administration, and hence damaged the cause of the South. No informed person would contend that Jefferson Davis was without faults; he had them. But the *Examiner*, in particular, was almost frenzied in its wildly irrelevant criticism.

The paper also attacked Secretary of the Treasury C. G. Memminger as "an aged spider, stuck in a dusty corner of the Treasury, ever busy, to excess, at weaving tangled, incomprehensible, but flimsy webs." Memminger was assailed and defended by various elements of the press, and finally resigned. The fact that the Richmond press could make such violent assaults on the government in wartime, without any effort by the authorities at suppression, is a tribute to their forbearance and their belief in the constitution.

Daniel's attitude toward events in the war was unpredictable. He was not impressed by the South's victories at Fredericksburg and Chancellorsville. At Chancellorsville Lee and Jackson had brilliantly defeated a much superior force, but Daniel sneered that the Federals were not destroyed either there or at Fredericksburg. These battles were like medieval tournaments, the *Ex-*

aminer declared, since the vanquished had merely suffered defeat, not destruction.

On the other hand, Daniel was not dismayed over the fall of Vicksburg, which placed the Union in control of the Mississippi River, or by the South's retreat from Gettysburg. The Confederacy hadn't gotten anything of value from the Mississippi, and the North would now have to divert forces to hold it, said the *Examiner*. As for Gettysburg, the Yankees were elated only because they hadn't been beaten as badly as usual.

Daniel kept a stiff upper lip publicly, and until the very end the *Examiner* professed to be confident of a Confederate victory. Actually, according to Hughes, "He was never very sanguine of the fortunes of the Confederacy, and in twelve or eighteen months after the war began had lost confidence in final success.... by the summer of 1864 he had lost all hope." Yet the *Examiner* proclaimed in September 1864: "If Richmond is held by the South until the first of November, it will be ours forevermore; for the North will never throw another huge army into the abyss where so many lie."

When Ulric Dahlgren's raid on Richmond in the spring of 1864 resulted in Dahlgren's death, the *Examiner* commented that his name was "linked with eternal infamy," and added that his body was given what it deserved: "a dog's burial, without coffin, pall or service." Papers had been found on Dahlgren's person that supposedly called for the assassination of leading Confederate officials.

When Northern targets were unavailable, Daniel never tired of abusing Confederate officialdom, especially President Davis. Most of these officeholders, for one reason or another, did not challenge him to a duel. Confederate Treasurer E. C. Elmore, a high-minded young South Carolinian, was an exception. When a scurrilous editorial appeared in the *Examiner* accusing him of being a gambler, unfit for his high office, he sent a challenge to Daniel. Daniel was never afraid of these encounters, even though after he received his wartime wound in his right arm, according to at least one account, he had to shoot with his left. The duel took place at 5:30 A.M., August 17, 1864, on Dill's Farm, Henrico County. This time Daniel was wounded in the leg.

Daniel was furious over the proposal, advanced that autumn, to enlist slaves in the Confederate forces in return for their future freedom. The blacks would be useless as soldiers, he contended, and they could not be better off than as slaves. But when, some months later, General Lee and the Virginia Military Institute backed the plan, he changed his position. By then it was too late to put it into effect.

Daniel lived in a three-story brick house on East Broad Street, opposite the African church. His work habits, personality, and appearance are charmingly described by George W. Bagby in his essay "John M. Daniel's Latch-Key." Daniel gave Bagby the key to his house in 1863, and Bagby, who was a contributor to the *Examiner*, was in the house frequently.

Daniel seldom went to bed before 2:00 or 3:00 A.M., and he rose belatedly; his breakfast hour was anywhere from 11:00 to 12:00. From then on, he was a dynamo of energy at the paper. Despite his delicate health—he was threatened with tuberculosis for years, and finally died of it—he did not spare himself.

He was a genius at editing other men's contributions and bringing them into line with his marvelously vivid style and his rancorous views. The entire paper bore his special cachet, despite the fact that much of the material was contributed by others. Among his contributors were such men as Patrick Henry Aylett, William Ould, A. E. Peticolas, L. Q. Washington, Basil Gildersleeve, John R. Thompson, and of course Edward A. Pollard, Robert W. Hughes, and Bagby. Nothing was signed, however, and although important material often came from persons not on the staff, when published it bore the editorial imprint of the master.

Without Daniel's touch, the *Examiner* languished. When he served briefly in the war and was wounded, and when he was wounded again in his duel with Elmore, the paper was conducted by others. It is no disparagement of those who replaced him temporarily, George Bagby wrote, "to say that the paper in their hands was never what it was in the hands of John Daniel." This was because "he had in him an intensity of bitterness which they did not possess; he had a strength of originality, an art of attracting contributions and of shaping them into his own similitude."

With regard to Daniel's literary style, Bagby wrote: "His pen combines the qualities of the scimitar of Saladin and the battle-axe of Coeur de Leon." Dean Swift was the writer whose style he most sought to emulate, with Voltaire a close second. Daniel was fluent in French, Italian, and Latin, and was widely read, with a tenacious memory. "He had little humor," according to Bagby; "he was too bitter for that. But he had the quickest and keenest appreciation of the humorous. Wit he had in a high degree, and of every sort." Daniel's outsized ego was obvious, and he told Bagby, "I love power; I like to command men." He often exhibited a grievous lack of consideration for his employees, but at times Bagby witnessed acts of great kindness and offers of financial aid. The *Examiner* paid the best wages of any Richmond paper. In his family relations, Daniel "treated his relatives with unkindness," Bagby said. Furthermore, "he never had a friend with whom at some time he did not have a misunderstanding."

Despite his predominantly sour personality, in his social contacts Daniel could be charming, on occasion. Mary Boykin Chesnut, the celebrated Civil War diarist, wrote that in 1863 she happened to sit next to him at dinner without knowing who he was. She thought him "clever and agreeable to the last degree." In the course of the conversation she remarked that she thought John M. Daniel ought to be hanged for his disruptive editorials which "are splitting us into a thousand pieces" and aiding the Yankees. He "looked grim" but did not identify himself. Not until later did she find out who her attractive dinner companion had been.

Daniel remarked near the end of his life that he was worth nearly $100,000 "in good money," and that the *Examiner* "is a very valuable property." And he went on to say: "When I am rich I shall buy the old family estate in Stafford County, and shall add to it all the land for miles around. I shall build a house to my fancy, and with my possessions walled in, I shall teach these people what they never knew—how to live like a gentleman."

"Whatever you do, don't be a preacher," Daniel advised his cousin, Moncure Daniel Conway. "It is a wretched profession. Its dependence is on absurd dogmas. The Trinity is a theological invention, and hell-fire simply ridiculous."

Daniel was, of course, an uninhibited defender of slavery. "The presence of an inferior race influences and *helps* to mould the manners and the character of the white man in the South," he wrote. "It inspires every citizen with the feeling of pride and decent self-respect.... White men, whether slave-owners or not ... behave with reserve, circumspection and dignity in the presence of the Negroes.... All history shows that slavery never did enervate national character, but has always strengthened and improved it." On another occasion he explained why slavery benefits the slave: "While living with the white man in the relation of slave, he is in a state superior and better for him than that of freedom."

As the war drew to a close, Daniel's frail health grew worse and he was sinking steadily. In the early months of 1865 most of the editorials were written by John Mitchel, an Irishman who came to the paper from the *Enquirer.* Mitchel "was under the strange hallucination that the Confederacy was then just on the

54

threshold of success and triumph." Even Daniel, who had expressed himself as being without hope, nevertheless was said, in his last hours, to have credited a rumor that Lee had crushed the whole Federal line in front of Petersburg. Pneumonia had weakened him, and an acute attack of his old nemesis, tuberculosis, carried him off. He died at age thirty-nine on March 30, 1865, as the Confederacy was collapsing about him. The last number of his *Examiner*, which appeared on the day before fire wiped it out, along with most of the city's business district, announced his death.

His vivid, scintillating and caustic, often ill-natured and surly editorials were widely read throughout the Confederacy, as well as in the North. Whether one agreed with them or not, they gripped the reader's attention in a manner that few journalists could equal. Utterly fearless, Daniel risked almost daily challenges, for he was never happier than when offering insults to prominent persons, especially those in public life. Some credited him with having had more influence than anyone in bringing about Virginia's secession, and despite his constant, carping criticism of President Jefferson Davis and his administration, he probably helped to maintain Southern morale when the South's fortunes were at their lowest.

Frank Luther Mott writes in his history of American journalism that "the *Examiner* was sometimes spoken of during the war as a 'school of journalism', because some of the most brilliant young Virginia writers contributed to it." But, as previously noted, Daniel was the one who gave tone to the whole operation, for the contributions of these writers were thoroughly edited by him, sometimes to the extent that they scarcely recognized their productions.

Whitelaw Reid, a young war correspondent with the Union army and afterward editor of the New York *Tribune*, wrote that "the newspapers of Richmond, throughout the war, were in many respects the ablest on the continent . . . and shaped the public sentiment of the whole Confederacy." Most original, most readable and most pungent of them all was the *Examiner*—with its cantankerous and churlish editor whose sparkling and irritating pronouncements made him famous in the annals of American journalism.

Edward A. Pollard, the vitriolic associate editor of the *Examiner*, was a suitable coworker for John Daniel. His attacks on Northerners were almost as intemperate as those of Daniel, and it was he who composed most of the paper's assaults on Jefferson Davis and Mrs. Davis. His views concerning Yankees may be glimpsed from the following: "We can never go back to the embraces of the North. There is blood and leprosy in the touch of our former associates." During the war he called for execution of Northern prisoners of war in retaliation for what he termed the North's crimes. Pollard's views were doubtless influenced by the fact that his brother had been killed years before in a duel by a Northerner whom he had challenged because of that man's aspersions on the South and slavery.

In addition to urging the execution of Northern prisoners, Pollard wrote that "enemy agents, deserters, counterfeiters, stragglers from the army, and blacks who had been behind Federal lines should all be put to death summarily."

An editorial in the New York *Tribune* in 1859, ridiculing Pollard—who was then in Washington—because of a tribute he had written to his black "mammy," must also have fueled his hatred of the North. The observation was the work of C. T. Congdon of the *Tribune*'s editorial staff, who delighted in needling the South on every possible occasion. The editorial said:

Wiping copious tears from his eyes, Mr. Pollard informs us that "in his younger days" he made "little monuments over the grave of his mammy." How many he made he does not inform us. What material he used, we are not told; but we know that infant architects have a partiality for mud.

And now Mr. Pollard, discarding the sentimental, waxes savage. Standing over the grave of his "mammy", and suddenly getting angry without any apparent occasion, he cries: "Do you think I would ever have borne to see her consigned to the demon abolitionists?" There is really no need for all this vehemence. We perfectly understand the case. We appreciate Mr. Pollard's feelings. We know he could not have borne it. For . . . had the demon abolitionists caught Mr. Pollard's "mammy", he is perfectly certain that they would have "consigned her lean, starved corpse to a pauper's grave." . . . Of all the poor white people in Washington, he seems to be in the lowest spirits—if we except President James Buchanan.

Pollard had a somewhat checkered early career. Born at "Alta Vista," in Albemarle County, he enrolled briefly at Hampden-Sydney College. Then he attended the University of Virginia from 1847 to 1849, after which he matriculated at the College of William and Mary. He was "given leave to withdraw" a few months after his arrival at the latter institution, and forbidden to return, apparently because he had "formed habits of gay living." On the eve of the war he was in Washington as clerk of the judiciary committee of the House of Representatives. He spent the years of conflict on the staff of the *Examiner*, until he was captured running the blockade in 1864, after which he was a prisoner of the North until shortly before the surrender. Soon after the end of the war, Pollard went to Europe briefly, but he returned and resumed his defense of all things Southern.

He and his family were involved in various gun battles, for gun play was amazingly frequent in that hectic era. H. Rives Pollard, Edward's brother, a wartime member of the *Examiner*'s staff, got into a shooting affray in 1868 which sent bullets whizzing around Houdon's statue of Washington at the Capitol, while the General Assembly was in session a few feet away. Nathaniel Tyler and William D. Coleman, both of the *Enquirer*, were the other participants in this incredible affair. All three men had gone to the Capitol armed, and when an argument broke out, they drew their pistols. "Mr. Pollard took his stand behind the statue of Washington and commenced firing," said the account in the *Dispatch*. His fire was returned by Mr. Coleman "with a single barrel pistol," whereas "Mr. Tyler did not fire." Nobody was hit, and the only casualty was the tassel on Washington's marble cane. Pollard was tried and reprimanded by the House of Delegates.

E. P. Brooks of the New York *Times* was in town and found the event so amusing that he wrote a humorous and ironic story for his paper. Pollard took such offense at this that he attempted to cowhide Brooks in the lobby of the Spotwood Hotel. The men got into a wrestling match and went through a plate-glass window.

Rives Pollard came to a violent end two years later. As editor of a journal called *Southern Opinion* he wrote something that a Richmond citizen, James Grant, took as an insult to his sister. Grant accordingly stationed himself in a second-story window across from Pollard's office at Fourteenth and Main Streets, and when Pollard appeared Grant poured a load of buckshot into his back, killing him instantly. Edward Pollard returned to Richmond from Baltimore to aid in Grant's prosecution, but had difficulty getting a lawyer who was willing to take the case. Rives Pollard was unpopular and considered "a gadfly," Jack P. Maddex, Jr., wrote in *The Reconstruction of Edward A. Pollard*. Furthermore, "the conservative gentry of Richmond . . . generally approved the deed," and "many who had witnessed the murder cheered." When Grant was tried, the jury took only forty minutes to acquit him. Edward Pollard was furious and he left Richmond, terming it "the wickedest city in America."

It would seem that the Pollard family had been involved in enough shooting to last several lifetimes, but now Mrs. Edward Pollard got into the act. Her husband had been absent from his Baltimore home for several weeks in 1868, and she suspected that his friend Dr. George W. Moore, a druggist, knew of his whereabouts. Moore said he didn't know where Pollard was, but Mrs. Pollard persisted in questioning him, until he became exasperated and ordered her from the premises. They scuffled and she drew a pistol and fired, hitting him in the wrist. "She was conveyed to the city jail to await further developments," said the *Dispatch*.

At about this time Edward Pollard underwent one of the most astounding metamorphoses that could well be imagined. After being for many years a defender of all things Southern, he turned abruptly into a savage critic of the Old South, slavery, and the Confederacy. As recently as the summer of 1867 he had been "as firmly wedded to proslavery separation as ever," and he "predicted resumption of the war," according to Jack Maddex; moreover, "he thought that black servitude could yet be restored in some form."

As an interlude during this period, Pollard was attacked with gunfire on the streets of Baltimore by two nephews of former Governor Henry A. Wise, who resented his criticisms of their uncle.

In *The Lost Cause Regained* (1868) and *Life of Jefferson Davis: With a Secret History of the Southern Confederacy* (1869), he repudiated many of his former views and made a quantum leap in the other direction. He was not only unsparing in his denunciation of Davis, as he had always been, but he turned on Robert E. Lee and Stonewall Jackson, saying that Lee was a poor strategist and Jackson a quite uninspiring character. Furthermore, said he, most Confederate soldiers had served under duress, half of them had deserted at the first opportunity, multitudes had evaded the draft, and so on. In addition, the South had been wrong to secede, and the Confederate government should never have been established. Pollard also extolled the Union in the highest, even adoring terms. Enfranchisement of the Negro was desirable, he now thought, and he blasted the Ku Klux Klan for "one of the vilest demonstrations of lynch law." However, he still favored white supremacy, with provisions for what amounted to second-class citizenship for blacks.

It was certainly possible for an individual to have changed his mind completely and honestly concerning some of these matters. Pollard left little room for doubt, however, as to the motives for his conversion when, in order to get a job in the New York customs house, he actually took the "iron-clad oath." In doing so the wartime associate editor of the *Examiner* swore that he had "not yielded a voluntary support" to the Confederacy, or encouraged its war effort! (Jefferson Davis might have privately concurred with the latter assertion.)

Pollard spent his last years in New York. There he published a number of books expressing his newly acquired views concerning the Confederacy and related matters. He contracted Bright's Disease and died of it after an illness of two years. He was forty-one years old. Confederate General D. H. Hill charged him with "the most stupendous, wholesale plagiarism ever perpetrated in the literary annals of the world." While this might seem to have been a somewhat extreme statement, it was not wholly without plausibility.

CHAPTER FOUR

THE COWARDINS OF THE *DISPATCH*

W hen the Richmond *Dispatch* was founded in 1850, to become the parent paper of today's *Times-Dispatch,* the proprietors, James A. Cowardin and William H. Davis, announced
that it would be "dedicated to news and eschewing political affil-
iation." This policy was followed for about a decade and was extremely successful; at the outbreak of the Civil War, the *Dispatch*
had acquired a circulation of some 18,000—more than all the
other Richmond newspapers combined.

But its nonpartisan approach was short-lived. One of the great
myths of Virginia journalism revolves about the notion that the
Dispatch contented itself throughout its existence with printing
the news, and that it seldom took a stand on anything controversial. In actuality, the onset of the war and the bitter contentions
of the postbellum era caused the paper to abandon completely its
"above the battle" policy. It urged secession before that fateful
move was voted, and in the years after the war it became a mili-

tant and unabashed champion of white supremacy, as well as a power in the councils of the Democratic party. Some of its editorial pronouncements were outrageous, but it made them.

When established, the *Dispatch* was the first penny paper to be published south of Baltimore. It was also one of the first papers to install a double-cylinder Hoe press, considered a significant advance, especially for a penny newspaper. It soon became the Richmond journal with the most complete coverage of the news, and this paid off in circulation and advertising.

James Andrew Cowardin, the brains behind the paper, was not only a good businessman but a talented writer as well. Although many of the editorials in the early years were written by Hugh Pleasants, brother of John Hampden Pleasants and an experienced journalist who had covered the state constitutional convention of 1829-30, Cowardin found time for some salient contributions. He not only dealt with serious subjects but was an amusing contributor on such topics as "The Old Virginia Ham" and "Old Time Virginia Fiddlers." An accomplished fiddler himself, in his writings on the subject he included vignettes of other devotees of the violin such as Thomas Jefferson, William Wirt, and William H. Cabell.

Cowardin was born in Hot Springs, Bath County, Virginia, on October 6, 1811. He was descended from Abraham Cowardin, of Dutch and Spanish blood, who came to Maryland in 1671. Abraham's son John settled in Bath County. Young James Cowardin grew up there, and in the 1820s worked in the composing room of a Danville newspaper. He then moved to Lynchburg, a notable hatchery of prominent journalists. Cowardin became foreman of the *Jeffersonian Republican* and wrote for it occasionally. In the middle 1830s he moved from Lynchburg to Richmond and became chief confidential clerk to Thomas Ritchie of the *Enquirer.* Although he and Ritchie did not see eye to eye politically, their correspondence shows that Ritchie became personally fond of Cowardin because of his "cheerful and willing spirit" and his "active and obliging disposition."

Cowardin harbored ambitions for a journalistic career of his own, and after several years with Ritchie he and William H. Davis bought the *Times and Compiler*, Richmond's oldest daily, from John S. Gallagher. In that era, relatively impecunious individuals could somehow buy or found newspapers—a far cry from the situation prevailing today. Cowardin and Davis apparently realized early on that the *Compiler* was not long for this world, and they disposed of their interest. Cowardin decided to try the banking and brokerage business, but journalism was in his bones, and in 1850 he and Davis joined in founding the *Dispatch*. It was a tough struggle at first. Aside from the fact that other papers were well established, rivalry between the Whigs and the Democrats was so keen that it affected the manner in which advertising was placed. Whigs tended to put their ads in the *Whig*, while Democrats leaned to the *Enquirer*. Since the *Dispatch* was not aligned politically, its revenues suffered accordingly until eventually the paper became so firmly established that it could not be ignored.

As editor and publisher of the city's leading newspaper, James Cowardin would seem to have rated the title of "colonel," which was often bestowed on prominent persons in the antebellum era whether or not they had any relationship to the military. But there is no record that this accolade came to him, although his son Charles, chief of staff to four governors, was indeed a colonel. The prevalence of colonels in those years is evident from an experience related by the English travel writer, George W. Featherstonaugh. He gives the following account of a conversation between a resident of Winchester and a ferryman:

"Major, I wish you would lead your horse a little forward," which he did, observing to the man, "I am not a major and you need not call me one." To this the ferryman replied, "Well, kurnel, I ax your pardon, and I'll not call you so no more." Being arrived at the landing place he led his horse out of the boat and said: "My good friend, I am a very plain man, and I am neither a colonel nor a major. I have no title at all, and I don't like them. How much do I have to pay you?" The ferryman looked at him and said: "You are the first white man I ever crossed this ferry that want jist nobody at all, and I swear I'll not charge you nothing!"

James Cowardin seems to have been a sturdy citizen, admired by his fellows and regarded as a genial and companionable friend with a keen sense of humor. A contemporary described him as "a very cultured and fluent conversationalist and a most interesting raconteur, in a word, as accomplished as he was able, patriotic and good." The same observer declared that Cowardin was "absolutely incorruptible," and that "for more than a quarter of a century he wielded a powerful pen and contributed as much as any man to the development of the Old Dominion." In 1853 he was elected to the House of Delegates from Richmond as a Whig, but he did not run for reelection. Cowardin never ran for public office again, preferring to devote his attention almost exclusively to the *Dispatch.*

He was married to Anna Maria Purcell, and they had six children. The family owned a beautiful country home near Greenbrier, White Sulphur Springs, where they lived during the first part of the Civil War. Cowardin then bought a farm near Richmond on Grove Road, later Grove Avenue, outside what were then the city limits, and the family remained there until the war ended.

The first home of the *Dispatch*, until flames destroyed it in the great fire of April 2–3, 1865, was at 3 Governor Street, just north of Twelfth and Main. By 1850, when the *Dispatch* appeared for the first time, Main Street was passable for several blocks west of Twelfth, whereas in earlier years gullies and swamps had barred the way beyond Eleventh. Between Sixth and Seventh Streets on the north side of Main, there was what Mordecai describes as "quite a rural and romantic spot . . . a steep hill and a little valley, shaded with forest trees; a spring, the water of which formed a pond for fishing and skating—the silence broken only by the singing of birds, the croaking of frogs or the sports of children." By the late fifties, however, it had become "one of the noisiest spots in the city—filled with workshops, with machinery propelled by steam for preparing all sorts of building materials in wood, iron, stone or stucco."

Also in the late fifties, posts a foot apart were placed at each entrance to Capitol Square, thus impeding the entry of the cows that had previously mooed there, and also making it extremely difficult for ladies with hoopskirts to pass. Just how the ladies got by the posts to attend the unveiling of Crawford's equestrian statue of Washington in 1858 is not made plain in the columns of the *Dispatch*. The cows were definitely not among those present.

While in the antebellum years the *Dispatch* was reluctant to express itself on most controversial subjects, it did not hesitate to defend slavery. In 1852, for example, it said editorially under the caption "Slavery an Economic Necessity": "The whole commerce of the world turns upon the products of slave labor. What would commerce be without cotton, tobacco, sugar, rice and naval stores? All these are products of slave labor. It is a settled fact that free labor cannot produce them in sufficient quantities to supply the demands of mankind." The foregoing "settled fact" has since escaped the notice of a great many people.

When Henry Clay died, the *Dispatch*, though "nonpartisan" politically, was lined in black for two days. It termed Clay a statesman of magnificent calibre. Similarly, on the death of Daniel Webster, the paper asserted that "the mightiest intellect of the age has succumbed to the only power that could paralyze its energies or destroy its activities."

With the inauguration of Abraham Lincoln as president, all nonpartisanship came to an end. The paper declared at once that there would be war and said, "The address of Abraham Lincoln inaugurates Civil War, as we have predicted." The *Dispatch* referred to Lincoln as "His sable excellency," asserted that "the demon of coercion stands unmasked," and went on to say, "We will stand in a solid phalanx in defense of the independence and sovereignty and the sanctity of Southern soil." Later the paper termed Lincoln "a vulgar tycoon." (The term *tycoon*, popularized in modern times by *Time* magazine, is here seen to have been in use long before Henry Luce's publication appeared on the scene.)

During the war, the *Dispatch* was "flamboyantly patriotic" and strongly supportive of the Confederacy's fighting forces. When arsonists set fire to the Tredegar Iron Works in 1861, it recommended a resort to lynch law. The paper termed Yankee soldiers "thieves and cut-throats." Paper and ink became scarcer and scarcer as the conflict progressed, and the *Dispatch*, along with the other papers, had to trim its sails accordingly. The paper shrank in size, the newsprint on which it was printed deteriorated drastically in quality, and the type became worn and difficult to read. Yet by the end of the war, the paper was said to have 30,000 readers.

The *Dispatch* was outspoken in defense of Richmond's Jewish citizens against charges that they were the principal speculators who profited from the conflict. It declared in February, 1864: "We are thoroughly disgusted in this age of universal speculation and extortion, with the slang of 'Jew, Jew', a cry akin to that of the practical pickpocket, when he joins the cry of 'Stop, thief!' to direct attention from himself." The paper also pointed out that most Jewish businessmen in Richmond were jewelers or drygoods merchants, and hence "had no part in the high cost of food and shelter." Governor Letcher stated that "the crime of extortion . . . embraces to a greater or less extent all interests—agricultural, mercantile and professional."

After the offices of the *Dispatch* on Governor Street were wiped out in the conflagration of April, 1865, it was not until December of that year that publication was resumed. Soon the *Dispatch* was again boasting that its circulation exceeded that of its six competitors combined. Its editorial policy, furthermore, was as outspoken as any. In those turbulent years the paper came to be recognized as the leading organ of the Conservative, later the Democratic, party. The paper erected a substantial building on the north side of Main at Twelfth. This imposing structure was finally pulled down to make way for the new parcel post building.

Immediately after the war, James Cowardin made Henry K. Ellyson, a two-term member of the House of Delegates and former Richmond sheriff, an associate as half-owner of the *Dispatch*. Ellyson was primarily concerned with the business management, while Cowardin was more involved with editorial matters. The editorial and reportorial staffs were kept busy in the hectic years following the war, when Reconstruction was imposed on the South. The *Dispatch* was aggressive in attacking the Northern "carpetbaggers" who swarmed in the land and the Southern "scalawags" who collaborated with them. Some of the carpetbaggers were sincere idealists, but others were unscrupulous swindlers. Horace Greeley, editor of the New York *Tribune,* described the latter genus as "stealing and plundering, many with both arms around Negroes, and their hands in their rear pockets, seeing if they cannot pick a paltry dollar out of them."

There were political conventions in Richmond in 1867 and 1868, with many blacks as delegates. Reporters for the Richmond press had a field day ridiculing these individuals, whose grammar was often not of the best, thanks largely to the fact that it had been illegal before the war to educate slaves. For example, the *Dispatch* quoted George Fayerman, a black delegate from Petersburg, as saying, "Dis convention is a equal convention, and we all has equal and illegal rights here."

Dr. Thomas Bayne, a garrulous Negro dentist from Norfolk, made his appearance at the Republican convention in April, 1867, and he would also be heard frequently and at enormous length at the constitutional convention that opened in December. Dr. Bayne was "pure African" in color and features, and he dressed in a black cutaway, spotless white cravat, and well-shined black shoes. He was small and bouncy. A former slave, he had served as a member of the city council in New Bedford, Massachusetts, after the war, and he seems to have been an intelligent individual, although reporters insisted on quoting him as using atrocious grammar. Two extracts from his remarks, as recorded in the *Dispatch*, follow:

"I arises to a pint of order, sir. I wants to know, sir, if members can git up here and speak in dis manner concerning members on dis floor, and cuttalin ther rights, sir, to speak on dis floor, sir. I deny the proposition of de gentleman, and states that I has rights to speak here."

And:

"But bein' as I was born in North Carolina, raised in Virginny, and lived in Massachusetts, I hasn't got no manners, except to speak when de chair states dat I has de floe. We isn't here, Mr. President, to vote at the constitution like at rabbits goin' thoo de fence—shoot it as it pass."

Reporters continually wrote that black delegates said "dat" for "that," and Bayne wanted them to know that "t-h-a-t didn't spell dat." He added that if any reporter wanted to "argue the principles of education, he had only to lay down the glove."

The *Dispatch* replied on the following day, saying "the doctor

68

mistakes us," and went on to state: "We mean nothing insulting by reporting 'dat'... and he will doubtless agree with us that there were enough 'dat-a' in the convention for the reporters to go upon." Next day, the paper found "the colored men infinitely superior to their white confreres" and added that "there were more brains in the colored leaders than in the white riff-raff."

The constitutional convention was denounced unsparingly by the *Dispatch*, which termed it "altogether monstrous in character, entirely incapable and untrustworthy." As for its chairman, Judge Underwood, the paper said, "That a man so obnoxious should be elected to preside over the body is not surprising," and "indeed, quite fitting, when we consider the components." It added that he was "a man whom no one speaks well of, that we ever heard—who has been charged with corruption by the most distinguished Radicals in the state." The convention was dubbed by the *Enquirer* the "Mongrel Convention," the "Kangaroo Convention," the "Black Crook Convention," and the "Bones and Banjo Convention." It also declared, contrary to fact, that the members of the convention were "illiterate vagabonds, many of whom could scarcely write their names."

These derogatory words may well have been true of some of the delegates, but certainly not of Dr. Bayne or several other blacks. Among the latter was J. W. D. Bland, evidently a man of exceptional intelligence. He was killed three years later in the Capitol Disaster when the floor of the Supreme Court caved in under the weight of a large crowd, precipitating hundreds to the floor of the House of Delegates forty feet below and killing sixty-two persons. William H. Davis, Cowardin's former partner at the *Dispatch*, was one of those who lost his life. Henry K. Ellyson, his partner at the time, whose attempt to be elected mayor was the subject of the court hearing, was among the injured.

The Underwood Convention, as it was known, was not without its tense moments. "Damned liar" and "damned scoundrel" were tossed about between hostile delegates, and on at least one occasion, when a member called another a "damned liar," both men grabbed chairs, bent on mayhem. Nearby delegates intervened, and there was no bloodshed. Duels apparently were not thought of, perhaps because the Yankees and Negroes in attendance were not accustomed to invoking the code duello, while the white Virginians in the hall doubtless regarded those "damn Yankees" as so far beneath them socially that a caning or horsewhipping was the only proper remedy. No such remedy was attempted, however, so far as is known.

The convention's attention was diverted in January, 1868, by the coming to Richmond of General Benjamin ("Beast") Butler. Butler was supposed to have "liberated" sundry silver spoons while occupying New Orleans during the war. Furthermore, when the New Orleans ladies jeered at the occupying Union troops, Butler issued this order: "When any female shall by word or gesture or movement, insult or show contempt for any officer or soldier of the United States, she shall be regarded and held liable to be treated as a woman of the town plying her Avocation." The storm of indignation that greeted this Butlerian ukase was of international dimensions. Needless to say, Butler was detested throughout the South.

His arrival in Richmond was hailed by the *Dispatch* with the following headlines:

BUTLER IN RICHMOND
RECEPTION AT THE DEPOT!
PROCESSION TO THE HOTEL!!
HE RECEIVETH COMPANY!!!
His Speech at the African Church

Delegate Liggatt offered the following resolution to the convention: "Resolved, that citizens are requested to observe more than

ordinary vigilance in the preservation of their plate and silver-
ware (sensation and laughter)."

The *Dispatch* observed that "there is effrontery in the appearance of this particular man here that could not fail to arouse a
generous indignation." The paper added that "even two of the
most able of the Radical members left the hall."

Another Richmond paper, commenting on Butler's appearance
at the First African Church, snickered as follows:

THE BEAST

Butler spoke, chairman Wardwell smiled, mob applauded.
Sublime occasion! Hen-roost and pig-sty thieves forgot their
avocation, and chickens and pigs for two hours slept in undis-
turbed security, while petty pliers of small trades vied with
each other in doing homage to the more successful rascal!

One of the most unscrupulous and evil of all the Radicals who
sought to chastise the white South was the Reverend James W.
Hunnicutt. He lived in Fredericksburg before the war, and was
not only a slaveowner but an advocate of secession. After the
South's defeat, however, this gentleman of the cloth emerged as a
violent critic of Virginia whites and a fiery advocate of wholesale
Negro enfranchisement. The New York *World*'s correspondent in
Richmond wrote of him that "none who gaze upon that countenance, so full of cunning and malignity, can ever forget it." The
New York *Times* declared that "it is time for good men of all parties to discountenance and disown him."

Hunnicutt presided over the April, 1868, Republican convention in Richmond, consisting of 160 blacks and 50 whites. In 1864
he had said that racial equality was neither possible nor desirable, but three years later he was taking exactly the opposite position. Yet by the time the constitutional convention met late in
the year, Hunnicutt was in bad odor with even the Radicals.

A political chameleon with no discernible principles whatever, Hunnicutt decided to run for Congress. He somehow hornswoggled the *Dispatch* into thinking that he was a changed man. The paper spoke glowingly of his "recent manly and just principles and conduct," and went on to say that he was "an angel of light compared to Porter," his opponent, whom it called "one of the worst white men that ever put his foot on Virginia's soil." It is impossible to believe that Charles H. Porter was worse than Hunnicutt. At all events, the latter failed to convince the public that he was any sort of angel, and he lost the election.

The Ku Klux Klan reared its ugly head in Virginia in the years immediately following the war, contrary to the statements of various historians who have contended that the organization did not appear in the state at that time. The Klan threatened to hang Hunnicutt from the tail of Washington's horse in Capitol Square and to clip "Dr. Bayne's superfluous tongue and ears." In the Yorktown-Williamsburg area Klansmen made a brief appearance with a view to terrorizing the blacks. A Yankee schoolteacher related the following concerning the hooded KKK: "One of them held out a skull to one of our men [a Negro], and asked him to please hold it while he fixed his backbone! Another in some way disposed of a whole bucket full of water; our Aleck ... asked how anyone could drink so much, and the 'sperit' cried aloud, 'Wait till you've been in hell for a year!' "

The *Dispatch* acknowledged the presence of the Klan in early 1868, when it published the following:

They have come. Indeed they have! The K.K.K.s and none else. There entered the *Dispatch* counting-room last night a man, or a monster, and laid upon the counter the advertisement to be found below. ... We beg the Klan to seek another medium for their communications. ...

K.K.K. Klan No. VII

Knights, Fires on the Raths—Moon 3rd Quarter. The hour is at hand. Meet in the arbor. Grand Centaur President W. N. S. Observe LSVIII. Degree. Knights be vigilant. Vidette on the outposts.

SHROUDED KNIGHT,
Klan VII.

The paper may have disliked the Klan, but it accepted the ad and did not attack the organization, contenting itself with requesting the KKK to use another medium thenceforth. Although the Klan's operations in Virginia at that time were relatively trivial, it is obvious that they continued until 1868, when they seem to have ceased. In the post–Civil War years the organization was concerned exclusively with frightening the blacks. It was not until the twentieth century that a revived Klan also began attacking Roman Catholics and Jews as part of the hooded organization's un-American racket. Yet anti-Jewish sentiment in the 1860s caused several New York insurance companies to announce that they would no longer insure "Jew risks." A protest meeting was held in 1867 at Temple Beth Ahabah, Richmond, attended by both Jews and Gentiles, and resolutions were adopted refusing to patronize the companies in question. The *Dispatch* commented:

> Insurance companies who have thus heedlessly given this insult have done that for which they should make the most ample reparation, or the outraged community is entirely justifiable in making them feel the consequences through the severe retaliation it is in the power of the injured to bear upon them. . . . It is an honor to them [the Jews] that they are

as sensitive about all matters relating to their faith, and as prompt to defend it, as any other in the world.

The Underwood Convention adjourned in 1868, after adopting a constitution which alarmed the white population of Virginia, since under its terms the blacks would almost certainly be given control of the state. As the vast majority were illiterate and without any sort of training for such responsibilities, it was an extremely disturbing prospect. The *Dispatch* thundered that the constitution had been forced upon the people of the commonwealth by "one of the vilest and most ruthless gangs of political marauders, corruptionists and malignants that ever disgraced a civilized country." Even General J. M. Schofield, the Union general in command of Military District No. 1, namely Virginia, realized before the proposed constitution was adopted that it would never work, since the plan was to "disqualify everybody in the state who was capable of discharging official duties," while giving "the Negroes and carpetbaggers full sway." Schofield, a high-minded man, appeared before the convention in opposition, but his advice was ignored.

Faced with the critical situation occasioned by the convention's adoption of the constitution, Alexander H. H. Stuart of Staunton, a member of President Millard Fillmore's cabinet before the war, took the lead in late 1868 in formulating a plan for what was termed "universal suffrage and universal amnesty." It provided that the whites would accept Negro suffrage if the disfranchisement and test-oath clauses banning nearly all whites from the ballot could be voted on separately in the popular referendum on the constitution's adoption. By winning the right to vote on the test-oath and disfranchisement clauses separately from the referendum on the constitution itself, white Virginians could approve the constitution and qualify for statehood without at the

Thomas Ritchie
—*Virginia State Library*

Artist's representation of Burr-Hamilton duel
—*Richmond Newspapers*

John Hampden Pleasants
—*Virginia State Library*

Slave auction, as depicted in London *Illustrated News*
—*Virginia Historical Society*

"Satisfaction," engraving from New York *Mirror*
—*Virginia State Library*

1829–30 Virginia Constitutional Convention. Thomas Ritchie,
clerk of the convention, is seated at the table in front, on the left.
James Madison is addressing the convention. Painting by
George Catlin
—*Virginia Historical Society*

"Tippecanoe and Tyler Too" parade in Philadelphia, 1840
—*Richmond Newspapers*

Richmond, from site of Hollywood Cemetery, about 1832–34,
from a lithograph made from painting by George W. Cooke
—*Richmond Newspapers*

John M. Daniel
—*Virginia Historical Society*

George W. Bagby
—*Virginia Historical Society*

James River and Kanawha Canal at Richmond, undated
drawing by J. R. Hamilton
—*Richmond Newspapers*

Canal boat
—*Richmond Newspapers*

James Andrew Cowardin
—Richmond Newspapers

Henry K. Ellyson
—Richmond Newspapers

Charles Cowardin
—Virginia State Library

Front page of Richmond *Dispatch* for
November 28, 1850. There was no news
reported on the page
—*Richmond Newspapers*

Front page for April 1, 1865, less than
two weeks before the fall
of Richmond
—*Richmond Newspapers*

same time endorsing the clauses, which they of course would never do. It was a farseeing and wise program.

A "Committee of Nine," headed by Stuart, was formed to promote the plan. It was published in the *Dispatch* and the *Whig,* but the *Enquirer* refused to carry it. A heated discussion followed. Many whites were violently opposed to the scheme, and some even termed it "treason." Ex-Governor Henry A. Wise attacked it as "a living lie, a base hypocrisy, and a disgrace to the Confederate living."

Stuart and his cohorts were not deterred, however, and the *Dispatch* was among their staunch allies. James Cowardin went to Washington with the Committee of Nine, which sought to explain the plan to President U. S. Grant and Congress. They did so, and both Grant and Congress expressed approval. Cowardin wrote a series of dispatches to his paper from Washington in support of the scheme, and was influential in obtaining the defeat of the objectionable clauses in the referendum. At the same time, Gilbert C. Walker, the Conservative candidate, was elected governor over the Radical candidate, Union General H. H. Wells. The Virginia General Assembly proceeded promptly to ratify the Fourteenth and Fifteenth Amendments to the U.S. Constitution, as demanded by Congress. Ratification signalized the termination of Reconstruction in Virginia, which came to an end in January, 1870. The *Dispatch* had played a constructive and highly important role in bringing about this happy result.

General William Mahone, "the Hero of the Crater," was an important factor here in alliance with the *Dispatch*. A few years later, however, they would be bitter enemies. That was when Mahone led the fight for "readjustment" of the state debt and sought political control of the state. Most of the blacks supported Mahone, and the *Dispatch* made every effort to defeat him.

William Mahone came out of the war as a major general with

a fine record, but he was only five feet five inches tall, weighed only about a hundred pounds, wore foppish military and civilian dress, and had delicately tapered fingers and a falsetto voice. He and Mrs. Mahone had thirteen children. His digestive apparatus was such that he had to take an Alderney cow and chickens with him on all his military campaigns. So fastidious was Mahone as to his haberdashery that his tailor said he would rather make dresses for eight ladies than one suit for the general. He was promoted to major general in July, 1864, on the express orders of General Robert E. Lee, following the spectacular and crucially decisive bayonet charge of Mahone's division at the Battle of the Crater.

The *Dispatch* feared that a political victory by Mahone meant "Negro rule," declared repeatedly that "no Negro is fit to make laws for white people," and cried "Shall we be governed by Negroes?" It also stated that "we would deprive them of no right; we merely wish to keep them in their own place."

Readjustment of the state debt of about $45 million—obligations incurred by the commonwealth before the Civil War—meant scaling down the debt, not repudiating it entirely. The argument for readjustment was to the effect that Virginia's economy had been wrecked and that most of the bonds for the debt were held in Europe—or in the North, which was responsible for the wrecking. A reasonable reduction in the debt was what was sought.

Recognized as the state's leading daily, the *Dispatch* allied itself with the so-called Bourbons, who felt that Virginia's honor was at stake and that every cent of the debt should be paid, even if the recently established public schools were left to starve. The *Dispatch* was relentless in its attacks on the U.S. Supreme Court and the subordinate federal courts for their rulings in the debt controversy, which the paper claimed were in direct violation of the Eleventh Amendment. The paper even argued that the country should rise and drive the judges in question from office. The campaign of the *Dispatch* against the courts had a wide impact both inside and outside Virginia.

The paper published a blacklist of Conservatives who had joined the Readjuster movement. It also hailed the "Thirty-Nine," a list of leading Virginians who formed a "society to preserve the credit of the state." It proclaimed that "the Conservative party is the white man's party, and the Radical party is the Negro party." The former, said the *Dispatch*, "proposes to keep all the offices in the hands of the whites, and the latter is *forced* to divide the offices with the Negroes." When some years later Mahone temporarily won control of Virginia with the aid of the black vote, he gave a few minor offices to the blacks, but there was nothing remotely approaching "Negro rule."

It should be said in all fairness that the *Dispatch* was not uniformly critical of the blacks and their institutions. For example, it was high in praise of the Negro Normal School, founded in 1867 by the Freedmen's Bureau for the training of common school teachers. The Freedmen's Bureau had been established by the Northern conquerors, but the *Dispatch* said, concerning the school's commencement exercises in 1873, "The examinations showed a degree of proficiency which would do honor to many schools whose pupils were more favored by previous conditions."

The paper also joined with other elements of the Richmond press in lauding the black companies of the voluntary state guard for their efficiency and good appearance. It praised blacks who presented the light opera "Pinafore" in 1880, saying that it was "very creditable when we consider the poor opportunities these people have had, and the very imperfect instruction the company received." The performance was before a mixed audience in the opera house.

Still more impressive was the stand taken by the *Dispatch* in 1886 on behalf of the participation of blacks on juries and in the

General Assembly, as well as their part in conventions and their riding in railway cars once reserved for whites. As C. Vann Woodward has shown in his *The Strange Career of Jim Crow,* the separation of the races in Virginia was much less rigid in the 1880s than it was in the postbellum years immediately preceding, or those which came soon thereafter.

We quote the editorial that appeared in the *Dispatch* on October 13, 1886:

> Our State Constitution requires all state officers in their oath of office to declare that they "recognize and accept the political and civil equality of all men." We repeat that nobody here objects to sitting in political conventions with Negroes. Nobody here objects to serving on juries with Negroes. No lawyer objects to practicing law in court where Negro lawyers practice.... Colored men are allowed to introduce bills in the Virginia legislature, and in both branches of this body Negroes are allowed to sit, as they have a right to sit. George Washington Cable, the aggressive agitator for the rights of Negroes, protested strongly against the discrimination elsewhere, but is authority for the statement, made in 1885, that "in Virginia they may ride exactly as white people do and in the same cars."

The situation thus described did not last. A reaction against black suffrage set in, and at the state constitutional convention of 1901–02, stringent requirements and restrictions were instituted. These too were favored by the *Dispatch.*

James Cowardin had died in 1882. A stroke in 1879 left him paralyzed on one side, but as a friend put it, "He was the same genial, kind, polite, considerate and simple-hearted Cowardin, abounding in anecdotes and incidents of the past." From 1882 on, his son Charles O. Cowardin was in charge of the paper.

Born in 1851, Charles Cowardin won an M.A. degree from

Georgetown College in Washington, now Georgetown University. He joined the staff of the *Dispatch*, and his first tasks were in the editorial rooms. Soon, however, he became primarily concerned with the paper's business side, although he remained in overall charge.

Charles Cowardin served as chief of staff for four governors— Lee, McKinney, O'Ferrall, and Tyler—probably a record, and was addressed as "Colonel." He was also president of the Westmoreland Club. Noted as a raconteur and after-dinner speaker, he was no less popular with the galley boys on the paper than with Richmond's elite. Charles A. Dana, the famous editor of the New York *Sun,* said "Charlie" Cowardin was "one of the brightest, as well as one of the sunniest men" he had ever met, and the *Sun* termed him "one of the two great storytellers of this century." Another paper said that on a trip to New York he had been "delightful, engaging, inimitable," and had sung "a ballad of his own composition." He was greatly talented as a musician and played several instruments. Active in the organization of the Mozart Association, he directed the choir of St. Peter's Catholic Church, as well as a number of amateur operas and operettas.

The *Dispatch* under his direction, and that of his father, was a great booster of Richmond and Virginia business, industry, and enterprise, and played a significant role in bringing the city and state out of the doldrums that followed the war. It was during Charles Cowardin's years as publisher of the *Dispatch* that Herbert T. Ezekiel, a member of the reportorial staff, witnessed an episode that demonstrated the independence of the paper from pressure by advertisers. A prospective customer wanted his ad published in display type and placed several hundred dollars on the counter in payment. But Cowardin was opposed to display type, and he objected. "Finally," said Ezekiel, "the money was shoved toward the customer, with the remark, 'Your money, my paper' and the publisher moved away." Since Colonel Cowardin was concerned primarily with the business side, a succession of editors functioned under him. William F. Drinkard became editor in 1882, served for several years, and was succeeded in 1887 by Henry K. Ellyson. On Ellyson's death in 1890, W. Dallas Chesterman took over.

The paper's remarkably objective comments on Negro rights and privileges in the 1880s, referred to above, were no longer heard by the end of the decade. The gradual reversal of opinion which took place in the city and state was reflected in the editorial position of the *Dispatch*. A flagrant example was the paper's comment in 1890 on John Mercer Langston, the black who was serving in Congress from Virginia. "While Langston is one of the best educated men of his race," said the *Dispatch*, "he is still a Negro, with all of a Negro's conceit, pomposity, credulity and stupidity."

In the same year, the paper went into virtual tantrums over the introduction into Congress of the so-called Force Bill, which provided for federal supervisors at the polls representing both parties when as many as five hundred voters requested it. The widespread fraud used in Southern states to prevent blacks from voting was the chief reason for this legislation. The *Dispatch* published a five-column, front-page editorial denouncing the bill. "Not for twenty years has the public mind been so disturbed," it declared. The bill was narrowly defeated in the U.S. Senate after passing the House.

The free silver issue, on which William Jennings Bryan would obtain the Democratic nomination for president in 1896, was espoused by the *Dispatch* with great enthusiasm in 1893. The country was in the grip of a severe depression, and many believed that free coinage of silver was the remedy. The paper urged a special session of Congress "to bring relief and renewed confidence to the people." Something like hysteria gripped large segments of the population who favored free silver. The Richmond *Times,* under Joseph Bryan, stood foursquare against the policy, and led in forming a group of Democrats firmly supporting the gold standard. Their convention was assailed by the *Dispatch* as not truly representative, since the three hundred delegates came from cities and towns rather than the country districts. Attempts by some gold Democrats to register black voters brought a charge from the *Dispatch* that they were trying to "Negrofy" Virginia. The defeat of William Jennings Bryan by William McKinley for president in 1896 put a virtual end to the agitation.

Dueling had become slightly less prevalent by the time Charles Cowardin succeeded his father in charge of the paper, and he never appeared on "the field of honor." He came close on one occasion, however. A bitter controversy with William C. Elam, editor of the Richmond *Whig,* the organ of William Mahone, brought a challenge, which was accepted. But before they could meet, the police got wind of it and arrested both men. They were placed under bond to keep the peace.

Colonel Cowardin's career was cut short at age forty-eight when he died in 1900 of typhoid fever. The Richmond *Leader* said that he gave "valuable service to public enterprises, for charity, for humanity, for party," and that he had "a heart full of love for God, humanity and country." He left a wife and four children. Few men of his time were so widely mourned.

The legacy of the Cowardins was a significant one. James Cowardin was a pioneer in the development of the news side of his paper, and in this respect he showed the way to his contemporaries. Furthermore, the editorial vigor manifested by the *Dispatch* after the first decade was, for the most part, used in constructive ways. It was an important factor in getting the commonwealth through Reconstruction with a minimum of damage, and in promoting industrial and business development. On the other hand, under both Cowardins the paper was excessively concerned with white supremacy, and except for one brief interlude, almost brutal in its references to Negroes.

James and Charles Cowardin were able and highly respected citizens, and their personal and professional contributions to the advancement of journalism and the interests of the white community were notable and lasting.

CHAPTER FIVE

GEORGE W. BAGBY—EDITOR, ESSAYIST, HUMORIST

Although George William Bagby's name is not identified with a particular Richmond newspaper or a particular set of views, no overview of the colorful scene in antebellum Virginia would be complete without a presentation of the career of this longtime newsman and humorist. Bagby was not only an able newspaper and magazine editor; he was also wartime correspondent for nearly a score of Southern newspapers, and a writer of delightfully humorous essays on various aspects of Virginia civilization. His fame was and is largely local, but inside the state he was, in some respects, in a class by himself.

Thomas Nelson Page termed him "next to Poe, the most original of all Virginia writers, master of a pathos rarely excelled by any author." John Esten Cooke declared that Bagby "exhibits a bizarre and original humor which is richer and rarer...than that of any other American." Joseph L. King, Jr., his biographer, to whom I am greatly indebted for what will follow, concluded after studying Bagby's whole career that "with the possible exception of William Gilmore Simms, no other man in the South touched so many phases of its cultural life, or worked harder to develop a literary spirit among its people."

Bagby was a humorist of almost unique stature, but at the same time an incisive commentator on the passing scene in editorials written before, during, and after the Civil War. A member of the editorial staffs of newspapers in Lynchburg, Richmond, Orange Courthouse, and Gordonsville, he also edited the *Southern Literary Messenger* for several years. In each of these capacities he made an impact and exhibited exceptional talent.

Bagby was renowned for his skill at portraying the antebellum Negro and his dialect. At the same time, however, he was sensitive to the feelings of the blacks. On this subject he wrote about his early days that "regard for the feelings of the Negroes, especially the older men, was strictly inculcated. Above all things I was taught not to call them Negroes, much less niggers, to their face. This was the unpardonable sin." He quoted one of his black friends as saying to him when he was a boy concerning his use of the word "nigger": " 'You good for nuthin', trifling owdacious scamp! Whar you manners? De ain't no sich a word—'taint in de Bible and you carn' fine it dar—and dar ain't no sich a word as nigger, ceptin' 'tis Niggerdemus, an' he warn' no cullud man.' "

Bagby was often addressed as "Doctor Bagby, " since he was an M.D. of the University of Pennsylvania. He practiced medicine for only a few months, however, before his remarkable gifts as a writer caused him to abandon it for a career in journalism and literature.

He was born in Buckingham County at the home of his mother, but he spent his early boyhood in Lynchburg, which he referred to as his home town. His father kept a general store there. Bagby was closely related to the Bagbys of King and Queen County, and specifically to those in and around the village of Stevensville. There was hardly anybody in Stevensville except Bagbys, and he described them as "hatchet-faced, white-haired pious Baptist folk . . . but by no means hard-shelled or rigid." He added that "they live in fine style and entertain handsomely." He himself never became a member of any religious denomination, but was inclined at one time toward Unitarianism. His wife and children were Episcopalians.

He began his education by attending several small private schools. An example of the type of primitive equipment and facilities available in some of these institutions is seen in his description of the one near Prince Edward Courthouse in which he was enrolled. Schooling was had in "one-third of a cinder-colored, weatherboard church which was pushed down the side of a hill to get it out of the way." After "instructing the youthful mind" on these premises six days a week, the Rev. Mr. Ballantyne, the headmaster, the top of whose head "was as bald as the bottom of a wash-bowl," used the other two-thirds of the rickety edifice for Sunday services.

At age ten Bagby was matriculated at Edgehill School, Princeton, New Jersey, which he described many years later as "second in reputation to no other school in the United States." None of the boys there was more than twelve years old, and the draconian regimen, compared to the relatively effete requirements of today, seems almost unbelievable. The little lads had to rise daily at 5:00 A.M. and wrestle with a curriculum which included Greek, Latin, mathematics, history, geography, philosophy, and religion. George did not get back to Virginia during his last two years at Edgehill until he completed his schooling in 1840. It was his journey homeward from Richmond to Lynchburg via the James River and Kanawha Canal at age twelve that he described long afterward in his delightful "Canal Reminiscences." As the youngest on board, he drew an upper berth, since "being light as a cork I rose naturally to the top." All went well until someone began to snore, Bagby wrote some forty years later.

> *Sna-a—aw——aw-aw-poof!, Sn-a-a-aw—poof! D* that fellow! Chunk him in the ribs, somebody, and make him turn over. Gentlemen, are you going to stand this all night? If you are, I am not. I am going to get up and dress. Who is he, anyhow? No gentleman would or could snore in that way!
>
> After a while silence would be restored, and all would drop off to sleep again, except the little fellow in the upper berth, who, lying there, would listen to the *trahn-ahn-ahn-ahn* of the packet horn.... How mournfully it sounded in the night!

Nothing could "keep a Virginian away from a julep on a hot summer's day," Bagby noted, and while the bar on board the craft was small, it was "vigorous and healthy." He was "then in the lemonade stage of boyhood," and he watched the Virginians inhausting their juleps: "Gentlemen, your very good health"; "Colonel, my respects to you"; "My regards, Judge. When shall I see you again at my house? Can't you stop now and stay a little while, if only a week or two?"; "Sam," (to the barkeeper) "duplicate these drinks."

When Bagby wrote the foregoing, the canal had succumbed to competition from the railroads. Looking back across the years, he sounded a nostalgic adieu to the "Jeems and Kanawha Canell," as it was often called:

> It knew Virginia in her palmiest days and it crushed the stage coach; isn't that glory enough? I think it is. But I can't help feeling sorry for the bullfrogs; there must be a good many of them between here and Lexington. What will become of them, I wonder? They will follow their predecessors, the batteaux; and their pale-green ghosts, seated on the

prows of shadowy barges, will be heard piping the rounde-lays of long-departed joys.

Farewell canal, frogs, musk-rats, mules, packet-horns and all, a long farewell. Welcome the rail along the winding valley of the James.

After that memorable trip on the "canell," the youth spent some time in Virginia, and then went back to school in Philadelphia—his father seemed determined to have him educated in the North. Then in 1843 he enrolled in Delaware College, Newark, Delaware. Not much is known of his two years there. He recorded that early in his freshman year "I had shown my manhood by smoking a pipe in Jesse Bouldin's room which made me sick as death." Also, he and seven others organized something called "The Knock-kneed, Bow-legged, Pigeon-toed Hyena Club," the machinations of which are lost to history. He "sparked" a few of the Newark girls and got wet when he broke through the ice on a mill pond, but seems to have made no memorable contributions to posterity at Delaware College.

After completing his sophomore year there, Bagby entered the University of Pennsylvania, at age eighteen. He emerged in 1849 with an M.D. and "a horrible dyspepsia from which I have never recovered." This serious digestive disorder plagued him for the rest of his life and probably affected his disposition. Although he was noted for his humorous writings and lectures, Bagby's was a far from effervescent personality. On the contrary, much of the time he seemed to be gloomy. Even when audiences roared at his most hilarious lectures, the speaker was absolutely deadpan and unsmiling.

Following his graduation in medicine, he went to Lynchburg but seems to have decided almost at once that medicine was not for him. He is said to have treated not more than half-a-dozen patients before turning to the more congenial profession of journalism. Early in the fifties the Lynchburg *Express* somehow came into the possession of Bagby, aged twenty-five, and his friend George Woodville Latham, aged nineteen. They conducted the paper for about three years, but since both were abysmally ignorant concerning the business side of a newspaper, it is hardly surprising that the whole thing collapsed.

Apparently Bagby's Lynchburg sojourn was free of violent happenings. The Lynchburg *Virginian,* a well-established paper founded in 1808, was then under the editorship of James McDonald. His predecessor, Abner W. C. Terry, had infuriated James D. Saunders with some critical words, and when the two met in the town market place in 1851, they drew their pistols and began firing. They kept on firing until both fell mortally wounded. But Bagby, who would himself challenge and be challenged to duels in the course of his journalistic career—although almost completely unschooled in the use of firearms—did not have any such experiences during his brief sojourn there.

McDonald, who was to aid Bagby at other critical times, invited him to contribute occasionally to the *Virginian* while he was editing the *Express.* He did so, and his first contribution, an editorial on Christmas 1854, revealed a talent for Rich, Beautiful Prose. Referring to the singing of the celestial choir, young Bagby wrote:

> The glad tidings of that blessed song seem to float over and through all time—through the wreck of empires—through the long night of the Dark Ages—through war, pestilence and famine, the overthrow of human hopes and human happiness—now dying away to the faintest echo, as died away the purity of the religion it heralded, anon rising as rose the Reformation, the restoration of letters, of arts, of liberty and morals—until in our day it rings out clear and high and joy-

ful, almost as when the "strain immortal issued from Angel lips."

With the solemnity of these recollections mingle others drawn from the history of our Anglo-Saxon sires. We recall the uproarious festivities of feudal times—the great castle filled with all that earth, air and water could supply; we can hear the "crackling laughter" of the immense "Yule log" as its flames go roaring up the wide chimney; the groaning table with its great smoking "Boar's Head" and its Wassail Bowl is present to our eye; the men at arms, the pages, the fool with his cap and bell, the maskers, the gleemen, the great lords and fine ladies.... And as that warm tinted picture of the good old times passes before us, we insensibly grow sad.

Where now are the brave lords and beautiful ladies, all who formed those joyous throngs? The worm has made his castle in the broad chest of the bold baron; the dust of centuries lies on the form and in the once bright eyes of the beautiful lady; the men at arms have laid down their armour; the songs of the gleemen are silent, and the sod is green on the grave of the fool. Even the stones of the castle have fallen, and the ivy trails its dark green leaves upon the wall and along the floor of the dining hall. The owl and the bat make merry there, and its only revellers are the dancing winds and the piping echoes....

Clearly Bagby had found his true profession.

Bagby was only one of a number of newspapermen who were trained in Lynchburg and afterward became well known. John Hampden Pleasants was the most conspicuous of these, but there were also James A. Cowardin and Robert Ridgeway, as well as Richard H. Toler, Page McCarty, Charles Maurice Smith, J. C.

Shields, and Addison Cole, along with James McDonald. In more modern times, Lynchburg was the birthplace of Douglas Southall Freeman.

While Bagby was struggling with the *Express* and dyspepsia, he visited frequently at "Avenel," the Burwell plantation outside Liberty, in nearby Bedford County. This typical rural Virginia home made a lasting impression upon him and was the inspiration for much of his later writing. His celebrated piece "The Virginia Gentleman," which appeared many years later, was based to a large degree on his observations of the life at "Avenel." " 'Avenel' and its inmates constitute one of the deepest and most beautiful parts of my life," he wrote in 1879 to Mrs. Bowyer, formerly Miss Kate Burwell. "They inspired the best writing I ever did and the only thing of mine that is likely to live."

Miss Burwell, for her part, described Bagby's appearance when he was visiting in her home during his years in Lynchburg: "He was a young man of slight but exquisite mould, dark, clear complexion, regular features, and eyes that had a depth and a beauty . . . gentleness and lambent fire combined—which made them unlike any eyes I ever looked into."

"Mountain View" near Farmville, the home of James Evans, his mother's brother, was another of Bagby's favorite places for relaxation and recovery. He spent more than a year there after the folding of the *Express* and battled his ailments. When he returned to Lynchburg in 1857 his health was greatly improved, although he would never be entirely well.

Bagby's rehabilitation at "Mountain View" had been retarded by the receipt of a devastating letter from a lady with whom he was deeply in love, informing him that she could not marry him. She was Miss Ellen Atwill Turner of Lynchburg, and the blow from "Blue-Eyes," as he was wont to address her, was a severe one. With characteristic humor, however, he wrote an article for a New Orleans newspaper entitled "Badly Kicked—Not by a

Horse." Bagby also contributed several articles to *Harper's* magazine during this period, evidence of his mounting success as a writer. The most notable of these was "The Virginia Editor," in which he provided a caricature of the swaggering, drinking, dueling scribe of the antebellum years.

The piece, which appeared in 1856, was shown in advance by the author to a number of his journalist friends, who appeared to regard the whole thing as good-natured raillery. But one of these was somehow persuaded after its appearance that he had been insulted and that he should challenge Bagby to a duel. He did so, and Bagby accepted immediately. The putative pistol-wielders set out for the famous dueling ground at Bladensburg, Maryland, and reached the scene ready to meet "on the field of honor." Suddenly Congressman Thomas S. Bocock arrived in headlong haste in a hack. A friend of both parties, he had learned of the challenge and resolved to stop the encounter, if possible. He succeeded, and there was a reconciliation.

Bagby left Lynchburg for good in 1857 when he obtained the position of Washington correspondent for the New Orleans *Crescent*. Soon he was also representing the Memphis *Eagle and Enquirer*, sending two letters a week to New Orleans and three to Memphis. It was a fascinating time to be in Washington, as relations between the North and the South worsened steadily and the country moved inexorably toward war.

Bagby's newspaper correspondence left him time for other writing. He contributed to the *Atlantic* and also produced the series of "misspelled" letters of *Mozis Addums to Billy Ivvins*. Eight of these appeared in the *Southern Literary Messenger* in 1858 and were an instantaneous hit. Indeed, they were so successful that Bagby was often addressed throughout the rest of his life as "Mozis," and there was a great demand that he produce additional communications from the semiliterate bumpkin whose observations on the Washington scene had the Virginia citizenry slapping their knees. The mode of misspelling humor, so popular in the mid-nineteenth century, is dated and somewhat incomprehensible to the modern generation, but Bagby's letters were widely reprinted and copied, and their author said he probably made more money from them than from anything he ever wrote. In addition, they increased the *Messenger*'s circulation by several hundred. Nevertheless, Bagby said he was sorry that he had created *Mozis,* since these productions were on a lower plane of literary endeavor then he aspired to, and he wanted to forget the letters and go on to higher things.

In 1859 Bagby returned to Richmond, which was to be his home almost continuously thereafter. He contributed editorials on a free-lance basis to local newspapers, and also served as librarian and corresponding secretary for the affiliated Virginia Mechanics Institute, Richmond Library Association, and Virginia Historical Society.

The first lecture he ever gave was delivered at this time in Richmond, and was entitled "An Apology for Fools." He was extremely nervous and his throat got so dry that, at times, he could hardly make a sound. "Add a small dog, who insisted on making my acquaintance," he wrote afterward. "Add, again a drunken man, who meandered slowly up to the stand, looked me full in the face, said in a thick, growling voice, but loud enough to be heard by half the house, 'Damn fool yourself!', and slowly meandered out again." He "pulled through somehow," he said, and "next morning I lugged a big silk handkerchief full of silver half dollars to the bank." While the money was welcome, he felt that the lecture had not been a success. He continued to deliver it, however, for three weeks in various parts of the state, and realized a sufficient sum to "spend a happy summer in Canada, New England and New York."

In June, 1860, Bagby became editor of the ailing *Southern Literary Messenger* at a salary of $300 a year, succeeding John R.

Thompson. Thompson had conducted the magazine as an almost exclusively literary publication, eschewing politics. But with the mounting tension between the sections, Bagby was one of the earliest of the militant secessionists and a scathing critic of the North. He also declared that defense of slavery was "defense of republican institutions," thus restating one of the more remarkable contentions advanced by the institution's defenders three decades before at the Virginia Convention of 1829–30. As for the Yankees, Bagby wrote that "not a breeze blows from the Northern hills but bears upon its wings taints of crime and vice, to reek and stink, and stink and reek upon the Southern plains."

Even before the Southern Confederacy was formed at Montgomery, Bagby was writing in the *Messenger*:

> By the life Virginia gave me, I know and I swear that our noble Mother will not be recreant to her fair fame, to her unsullied honour. Never, never, never will she consent to the shame, the infamy, the everlasting disgrace of joining the Abolitionists. It is not among the possibilities for Virginia to play the deserter—to sneak away from her friends and to creep abased and trembling into the camp of her enemies.... Let us fight for our wives, our children, our aged sires, whom the mercenary hordes of the North would fain deliver over to the sword of the invader and the pike of the Negro insurrectionist.

Once the Confederacy was formally established, Bagby was outraged over Virginia's dilatoriness in deciding to join her Southern sisters. While the Virginia Convention debated the matter, he continued to urge secession. Finally, after Lincoln's call for 75,000 volunteers to put down the "rebellion," Virginia seceded, and Bagby was enraptured.

Despite his frail physique and his chronic dyspepsia, he enlisted at once as a private. In his amusing essay "An Unrenowned Warrior," Bagby described some of his experiences and reactions to the military life, and especially his being drilled by a fat VMI cadet:

> To get up at dawn to the sound of fife and drum, to wash my face in a tin basin, wipe on a wet towel, and go forth with a suffocated skin and sense of uncleanness to be squad-drilled by a fat little cadet, young enough to be my son. . . . that, indeed, was misery. How I hated that little cadet! He was always so wide awake, so clean, so interested in the drill; his coat tails were so short and sharp, and his hands looked so big in white gloves. He made me sick.

Having weathered this ordeal, the "unrenowned warrior" was ordered to the vicinity of Manassas, where the opening engagement of the war was about to take place. There is a widespread impression that Bagby slept through the Battle of First Manassas, which took place on July 21, 1861, but such is not the case. That would have been almost too good to be true. What happened, according to his own account, was this. He noted on the night of July 17 that a lad of sixteen was serving as night orderly, and was unhappy over doing so. Bagby generously offered to take his place, and the youngster was grateful. "So I played night orderly from 12 o'clock till 6 A.M. thenceforward, and on that account slept the longer and harder in the afternoon," he wrote.

> Near sunset of the 18th I arose . . . washed my face and walked out on the porch. It was filled with officers and men, all looking toward Bull Run.
> "That's heavier firing than any I heard in Mexico."
> "It was certainly very heavy," was the reply, "but it seems to be over now."
> And that is all I know about the battle of the 18th. I had slept through the whole of it!

This, however, was not the major battle; it took place three days later. When that engagement occurred, Bagby was charged with the duty of looking after "the papers of the office, which had been hastily packed up, and, in case of danger, see that they were put on board a train, which was held in readiness to receive them."

Bagby walked out repeatedly to watch the fighting at a distance, and when he could stand it no longer, he "left important papers, etc. to take care of themselves, and set out for the battle-field, determined to go in and get rid of my fears and doubts by action." But the firing ceased, "a shout of victory went up," and he returned to headquarters.

He was annoyed that there was no "forward movement upon Washington" on the day following the battle. He did tell of an experience on that day which he believed could have affected his whole future career, but didn't. Private Bagby saw President Jefferson Davis come out of his tent, and he wrote that if he had made Davis's acquaintance, it would have been "a turning point in my life." Since a great victory had taken place, "it would have been an auspicious time to ask favors," and Davis was "very responsive to personal appeals." The orderly reasoned that he "could have become a member of his political and military family, or, what would have suited me much better, have gone to London, as John R. Thompson afterwards did, to pursue in the interest of the Confederacy, my calling as a journalist. . . . I could not force myself to open my lips, but walked back to my chair on the open porch, and my lot in life was decided."

In view of Bagby's bitter hostility toward Davis not long thereafter, and his constant criticism of him, it is difficult to picture him as "a member of his political and military family." But he seemed to believe that it would have been possible, had he summoned up the nerve to speak to the Confederate president after the Battle of First Manassas.

Following some weeks of idleness there, and much boredom,

Private Bagby was ordered to accompany the body of Lieutenant James K. Lee to Richmond. "In view of my infirm health," he wrote, "a discharge was granted me after my arrival in Richmond, and thus ended the record of an unrenowned warrior." Summing up his attitude toward the war, Bagby said he was willing to die for the South, "but not by freezing, and worse still, by filth." And he went on: "War is simply horrible. The filth, the disease, the privation, the suffering, the mutilation, and above all, the debasement of public and private morals, leave to war scarcely a redeeming feature."

Bagby's contributions to the cause of the South were made on another front, namely, in the field of journalism. In making them he worked long hours and did a tremendous amount of writing— as associate editor of the Richmond *Whig* from 1863 to 1865, contributor to the Richmond *Examiner,* editor of the *Southern Literary Messenger* until 1864, and correspondent for almost a score of Southern newspapers. Just how a man with so many health problems could have managed all this is hard to understand. However, he needed the revenue desperately as the war wore on.

Bagby joined with others in sneering at General Robert E. Lee in 1861. Following Lee's unsuccessful West Virginia campaign, when he was asked to achieve the impossible, Bagby wrote that "the people . . . will demand that the Great Entrencher be brought back and permitted to pay court to the ladies." He changed his opinion of Lee soon thereafter, as did practically everybody else. His more considered opinion was that Lee was "the stateliest man of all our time."

But Bagby never let up in his criticism of Jefferson Davis. On March 12, 1862, he wrote in his notebook:

We have reached a very dark hour in the history of this struggle. I do not say that the cause will fail, but the chances are all against us. The fall of Donelson and Nashville, the defeat of Van Dorn and Price, and the capture of New Madrid, are but small items if the people retained confidence in the president. . . . Cold, haughty, peevish, narrowminded, pig-headed, *malignant,* he is the cause of our undoing. While he lives, there is no hope for us. God alone can save us. . . . All hell will be in carnival when the Yankees triumph.

The Davis cabinet also felt Bagby's wrath. In the *Southern Literary Messenger* he termed Judah P. Benjamin "the chief thief in a cabinet of liars." As for the cabinet as a whole, he wrote later that it was "composed of a set of old fogy, broken down politicians who act as mere *clerks* to the president."

Such rancorous judgments were not only quite unfair, but very much out of character for a man of Bagby's usually kindly disposition. They were in line with the views of John M. Daniel and Edward A. Pollard of the *Examiner.* Davis was far from popular during the war. His style of leadership was not appealing to many Southerners. He had serious health problems, like Bagby, which made him irritable and peevish. He also suffered the loss of a beloved five-year-old son who fell from a Confederate White House balcony and was killed. As for the Davis cabinet, some members were better than others, but Bagby's overall characterization was far from justified, and neither was his libelous description of Judah P. Benjamin.

Bagby interpreted other phases of the Confederate war effort much more favorably. It is impossible to identify his editorials in the *Whig* and the *Examiner*, but it may be assumed that he made every effort to promote the cause of the South, in which he believed so deeply. In his correspondence for a score of newspapers, he interpreted events in Virginia for a broad Southern audience, and did so with great ability and exceptional knowledge. A Florida editor described him as "literally the best newspaper writer in the Confederate states."

John M. Daniel, who knew good writing, told Bagby when he went to Manassas at the outbreak of the war that he could name his price for anything he sent the *Examiner* from that theater. Bagby submitted one piece, which Daniel praised but didn't publish. In 1863 Daniel invited him to become assistant editor of the *Examiner,* but Bagby declined since he was already serving the *Whig* in a similar capacity. Bagby agreed to furnish Daniel "with two or three editorials a week," and he did so for several months. Daniel was so great an admirer of Bagby that he gave him a latchkey to his house, and this key, years later, became the subject of one of Bagby's most important essays. It is quoted at some length in the chapter on Daniel.

Plagued by poor health, insufficient financial resources, and a crushing burden of work, Bagby was under a severe strain throughout the war years. He survived, however, and managed to relax occasionally with members of what was known as the Mosaic Club—a group which gathered informally at one another's homes when members were back from the front. There was no fixed program for these meetings, which were relished especially when someone had a bit of real coffee or perhaps another rare delicacy. Innes Randolph is said to have tried out an early version of "The Good Old Rebel" before the club. "Jeb" Stuart was present on occasion, with his rich baritone, as was John Esten Cooke, a member of his staff. John Hampden Chamberlayne, later editor of the Richmond *State,* and described as "colossal in originality," and John Pegram, "a delightful and artistic whistler," were also participants when they could get away from the fighting. Page McCarty, who later fought the famous duel with John Mordecai over the fabulously beautiful Mary Triplett, was occasionally present. Miss Mattie Paul regaled the group with her virtuosity on the piano. Bagby's modest editorial sanctum was another rendezvous for congenial spirits from time to time. Termed "the Will's Coffee House of the war wits," it was a place where he and others scribbled bits of light verse on his cartridge-paper table-cloth.

In February, 1863, the thermometer hit ten below zero, and not only was the James River frozen hard; so was the ink in Bagby's inkwell. The year was an important milestone for Bagby, for he was married then to Lucy Parke Chamberlayne, the lovely and talented daughter of Dr. Lewis Webb Chamberlayne, one of the founders of the Medical College of Virginia, and his wife, the former Martha Burwell Dabney. Bagby had become acquainted with Miss Chamberlayne, the sister of John Hampden Chamberlayne, at one of the meetings of the Mosaic Club. Inflation was rampant at that stage of the war, but the newlyweds somehow managed a trip to Prince Edward, Buckingham, Lynchburg, and Charlottes-ville. The groom wrote later that on the journey he wore "a hand-some overcoat borrowed from John R. Thompson" and "sported a weak-necked meerschaum pipe which Ad. Williams had pre-sented him."

Their first child, Virginia, arrived in January, 1864, as the for-tunes of the Confederacy declined and Bagby became increas-ingly discouraged over the chances for victory. The child was sickly and so was her mother. Such cares and tribulations, when added to his own poor health and his staggering burden of work, almost broke Bagby down. But he not only carried out his respon-sibilities as editor and correspondent; he even produced a number of his better-known humorous sketches, such as "My Vile Beard" and "My Uncle Flatback's Plantation."

In May, 1864, as Grant was crossing the Rapidan, bent on driv-ing through to the Confederate capital, Bagby wrote in an out-of-town paper that Richmond "looks almost deserted," and he added:

Picture the closed stores; the almost empty streets; long trains of ambulances going to the depot; file after file of slightly wounded soldiers marching from the receiving to the regular hospitals; hearses going to Hollywood; funeral escorts preceded by a band of music, carrying the remains of general officers to the Capitol; soldiers bivouacking and horses grazing in the Capitol Square; the distant cheering of regiments marching to various points around the city, and you have a pretty fair idea of Richmond at the present time.

In another letter the following month he wrote: "Richmond begins to look seedy. A Yankee prisoner, brought the other day to the Provost Marshal's office, looked around and exclaimed 'Wal! this is a darned sorry lookin' place to fight so much for.' "

Only a few days before Richmond fell, Bagby and a dozen others gave a supper at the Ballard House for his longtime friend George Woodville Latham, with whom he had operated the *Express* in Lynchburg years before. "We all knew that the last great struggle was at hand," Bagby wrote. "Supper ended, we called with one voice for a song." Bagby described Latham's response:

He drew himself up to his full height. . . . his eyes blazed, his cheeks flamed and his power came back full tide in a torrent of fire, as he sang "Bruce's Farewell." It was what our hearts had wanted to hear, and it came with a grandeur, a death-defying patriotism, a might, a pomp and splendour of inspiration that dwarfed the "Marseillaise" itself. . . . It made the veins burn, and the heart ache to fight. It was a burst of true musical genius and power, such as few men have ever witnessed. . . . Carlyle (I think it was) tells the circumstances under which Burns composed that song, and says it ought to be sung by the throat of a whirlwind. . . . Would to God that every man in the Confederacy could have heard that glorious voice, and gone to battle the instant after.

But it was too late. The Confederacy was collapsing. Richmond had to be evacuated, and the ailing Bagby obeyed his equally ailing wife's injunction to "follow the Confederate fortunes as long as there is any Confederacy." He boarded a coach on the Richmond and Danville Railroad with members of the government and others, and they all got off at Danville. Mrs. Bagby and the child, also sick, remained in the city when, as Bagby wrote, "the awful fire was raging, when fragments of shell were raining on top of our little home, when the houses across the street were in flames, and when our own house, on fire a dozen times, threatened to burn down over their heads." He got back from Danville some weeks later, apparently by walking most of the 120 miles.

With Richmond devastated and jobs virtually nonexistent, Bagby decided to try his luck as a writer in New York, but after arriving there, he found that his eyes were inflamed and writing was out of the question. He returned to Richmond, and Mrs. Bagby gave birth to another child. She was extremely unwell, as was Bagby. Nobody seems to know how they managed to survive financially for the next few months. But they made it somehow, and Bagby concluded that his only prospect for earning an income was on the lecture platform. He put together a humorous disquisition called "Bacon and Greens," and with much trepidation delivered it in Lynchburg. It was an instant success, and invitations poured in from all over Virginia, as well as Washington, Baltimore, and New York. Even so, it was no bonanza, for his admission fee was twenty-five cents; if he cleared ten dollars for the evening, he was satisfied; if twenty, he felt that he was almost wallowing in opulence.

His eyes improved, and he resumed writing. One of his editorials made certain statements concerning prisoners of war that caused a Northern officer to question his veracity. Bagby challenged him at once to a duel, but the Northerner declined.

In 1867 Bagby formed a partnership with A. F. Stofer of Orange Courthouse in the publication of a weekly newspaper, which

The bail bond guarantee for Jefferson Davis's release from federal prison, signed May 13, 1867. Among the signatures are those of Gerrit Smith, Horace Greeley, Cornelius Vanderbilt, and other prominent Northerners

—*Virginia State Library*

they named the *Native Virginian*. He was in charge of the editorial side, while Stofer presided over the business office. In time they moved to nearby Gordonsville, which Bagby dubbed "the chicken-leg center of the universe," since for generations fried chicken was sold on the railroad station platform by blacks. After about three years, they abandoned the operation. Bagby wrote of the experience: "Stofer and I published the paper for a good long time, affording small buyers an abundance of cheap, but not very clean wrapping paper, and annoying the editors throughout the state by incessant personalities and political inconsistencies. . . . We gradually ran up our list to three hundred and fifty, including exchanges and copies given to friends on the cars."

In 1870 Bagby's friend James McDonald, who had become secretary of the commonwealth following Gilbert C. Walker's election as governor, appointed Bagby assistant secretary of the commonwealth and state librarian. This was a great boon to him, and enabled him to begin writing again for the best newspapers and magazines. He also resumed lecturing, seeking to raise money for the Virginia Historical Society and the Southern Historical Society while also supplementing his own meager income.

In 1878 General William Mahone's Readjusters gained political control, and Bagby was ousted from his job with the state. He had fought Mahone for years. With a wife and six children to support, the loss of his position as librarian made it necessary for Bagby to resume free-lance writing and lecturing on a full-time basis. Subsequently he wrote an able series of letters from around Virginia for the Richmond *State,* edited by his brother-in-law, John Hampden Chamberlayne.

"The Old Virginia Gentleman," his celebrated picture of life in the Old Dominion before the war, was written at this time. It "probably won for its author a wider reputation and a more enduring fame than anything else he ever did," says his biographer, Joseph L. King, Jr. It was delivered widely as a lecture and also published. High praise came from all over the state and beyond. Kate Bowyer of "Avenel," née Burwell, wrote him that when she read it to a group of friends, "everybody present was in tears— not a soul . . . able to utter a word for many minutes." Humor and pathos are beautifully combined in this masterly depiction. It is by no means a completely laudatory picture; Bagby himself said that he included "a full proportion of good-natured satire," and he went on to say, "Educated at the North, I was perhaps more keenly alive to the defects of our system than almost any Virginian of my time."

A few extracts from "The Old Virginia Gentleman" will serve to give the flavor:

On the first day of December, 1763 Patrick Henry made his speech in the Parson's Cause, and after the convention of 1829–30, the giants no longer assembled in Virginia. I will put the breed of human animals reared in this interval, less than a century, out of a free, male population not exceeding that of Attica, against any other ever produced in the world. I doubt if the Roman Senate or the Athenian Areopagus ever at one time contained quite such a body of men as was gathered in our famous convention, and I will say . . . that we have not now, nor are we likely ever again to have, two such men as Washington and Jefferson. . . .

A murrain on your modern reapers and mowers! What care I if Cyrus McCormick was born in Rockbridge County? These new-fangled "contraptions" are to the old system what the little, dirty, black steam-tug is to the three-decker, with its cloud of snowy canvas towering to the skies—the greatest and most beautiful sight in the world. I wouldn't give Uncle Isham's picked man, "long Billy Carter" leading the field, with one good drink of whiskey in him—I wouldn't give a swing of his cradle . . . for all the mowers and reapers in creation.

The house of the Old Virginia Gentleman was "on the main, plain road," but out of sight.

And what was to be seen on the main, plain road? Nothing. Morning and evening the boys dashed by on their colts, hurrying to and from the Academy, so-called. On Sundays, carryalls, buggies and wagons filled with womenfolk and children, wended their way to Mt. Zion, a mile or two further in the woods. Twice a week the stage rattled along, nobody inside, and a Negro in the boot, the driver and the Negro trader, both drunk, on top. Once a month the lawyers, in their stick-gigs or "single-chairs", and the farmers on their plantation mares, chattering and spitting amicably . . . jogged on to court. And that was all that was to be seen on the main, plain road.

The foregoing extract is an excellent example of Bagby's unwillingness to glamorize the antebellum South. He was a realist who usually took pains to describe the old life as it was, rather than as romantically and glowingly depicted by Thomas Nelson Page and John Esten Cooke. Cooke was a friend of his, but Bagby wrote that he had eyes only in the back of his head, and they were colored with rose-tinted glasses of tremendous magnifying power. "The respectable gentlemen and ladies who were buried down at Williamsburg about eighty years ago," Bagby declared, "were, I doubt not, very nice people, but they are too dead for my taste." He went on to say that he could not understand how "such a set of homely, selfish, money-loving cheats and rascals as we are, should have descended from such remarkably fine parents. No doubt it is very good noveling, but it is wretched physiology."

The most widely known of all Bagby's writings in his own day was "Jud Browning's Account of Rubenstein's Playing." Written during the same period, it has appeared in school textbooks on both sides of the Atlantic, frequently with the words "Author Unknown" appended. Bagby apparently never got a cent for it; nor is there any certain knowledge as to the newspaper in which it first appeared. This is an extraordinary example of onomatopoeia, the formation of words in imitation of natural sounds. Bagby's description of Rubinstein's magic with the keyboard (he misspelled the pianist's name) is remarkably imaginative. The piece is entirely too long for complete quotation here, but the following extract affords at least a glimpse of its exceptional qualities:

He tweedle-leedled a little on the trible, and twoodle-oodle-oodled some on the base—just foolin' and boxin' the thing's jaws for bein' in his way. . . . I heard a little bird waking up away off in the woods, and calling sleepy-like to his mate. . . . It was the peep o' day. The light come faint from the east, the breeze blowed gentle and fresh, some more birds waked up in the orchard, then some more in the trees near the house an' all began singin' together. . . . The next thing it was broad day, the sun fairly blazed, the birds sang like they'd split their little throats. . . . Presently the wind turned, it began to thicken up, and a kind of gray mist come over things. . . . Then a silver rain began to fall. . . . Then all of a sudden old Ruben changed his tune. He ripped and he rar'd, he ripped and he tar'd, he pranced and he charged like the grand entry in a circus. . . . He lit into them keys like a thousand of brick. . . . He changed his tune again. He hoptlight ladies and tiptoed fine from eend to eend of the keyboard. He played soft and low and solemn, I heard the church bells over the hills. The candles in heaven was lit, one by one. . . . Then he got mad. . . . he just went for that old pianner.

He slapt her face, he boxed her jaws. . . . till she fairly yelled. . . . He fetcht up his right wing, he fetcht up his left wing, he fetcht up his center, he fetcht up his reserves. The house trembled, the lights danced, the walls shuk, the floor come up, the ceilin' come down . . . raddle-addle-addle-addle—riddle-iddle-iddle-iddle—reetle-eetle-eetle-eetle-eetle-eetle—p-r-r-r-rlang! per lang! per plang! Bang!

With that *bang!* he lifted himself bodily into the a'r, and he come down with his knees, his ten fingers, his ten toes, his elbows and his nose, striking every single, solitary key on that pianner at the same time.

In 1880 Bagby visited Connecticut as a representative of the Baltimore *Sun* and wrote twelve articles. For one who had excoriated the Yankees before and during the war in blistering prose, his writings from New England were in startling contrast now. He wrote that he "learned that the Southerner, not the Northerner, was most guilty of hard feelings," and was "deeply moved" when "one speaker after another" at a gathering on the New Haven common defended the South. "The Yankees are more like ourselves than we are willing to believe," he wrote. Bagby was happy that on his journey he encountered "no sniveling divines." He also paid tribute to the thrifty propensities of the Connecticut citizenry: "There is a marked difference between the spitting of Yankees and the spitting of Southerners. Economical even in his expectoration, the Yankee holds the quid half a day, ejecting at long intervals a meagre drop or globule, rarely squirting, never spattering. . . . The very salivary glands of these people are labor-saving." Tobacco chewing was so widespread before and after the Civil War that somebody suggested that the national emblem should be the spittoon rather than the American eagle. Charles Dickens was appalled on his visit to America in 1842 by the "perfect storm and tempest of spitting" on a Pennsylvania canal boat.

Richmond did a tremendous business in the manufacture of plug tobacco.

Bagby followed up his series in the *Sun* with another gesture for intersectional reconciliation. He accepted an invitation to speak in Trenton, New Jersey, and called his address "Yorktown and Appomattox: A Plea for Peace." He spoke of the "Temple of Concord, a House of Peace, stately and fair as the amity and the brotherhood that designed it; grand as the united people that build it; enduring as the nation that ordains it." On this lofty note, George W. Bagby ended his public career. It was his last address, for his health began to decline. Cancer of the tongue caused him excruciating pain, and his sufferings were agonizing. Relief came with death on November 29, 1882. He was fifty-five years old.

Bagby's name today is far from a household word, even in Virginia, but he deserves to be remembered. He was never able to write the book on Virginia that he planned, but his briefer pictures of life there in the antebellum era are among the most delightful that we have. His humor and pathos moved his readers to laughter and then to tears. The lectures that he delivered all over the state were among the few bright spots that illumined the years following the South's defeat.

The ordeals and sufferings that he endured throughout much of his adult life were met with great fortitude. Burdened with serious health problems and equally serious financial problems, as well as almost constant nervous tension and occasional eye trouble, he carried on in the face of obstacles that would have daunted a less courageous man. Outwardly he often appeared gloomy, especially in his public addresses, despite his humorous sallies. Thomas Babington Macaulay wrote of Dean Swift, another humorist, that "all the company are convulsed with merriment, while the Dean, the author of all the mirth, preserves an invincible gravity." It was equally true of Bagby.

Douglas Southall Freeman wrote that George William Bagby "made Virginia smile in its time of sorrow," and that he "is to be included in any intelligent list of the half-dozen men who did most for Virginia in the years immediately following the war." Bagby, who loved Virginia as few men did, would have been justifiably proud of that well-deserved tribute.

CHAPTER SIX

CAMERON, CHAMBERLAYNE,
ELAM—AND MAHONE

Virginia editors in the postbellum era had to contend with a squeaky-voiced, hundred-pound former Confederate major general with marked dictatorial propensities. He was William Mahone, "the Hero of the Crater," who had much to do with keeping Virginia in turmoil for two decades after the end of the Civil War. You were either for Mahone or against him. Many were convinced that he was an everlasting threat to the well-being and the traditions of the commonwealth. Others agreed with one of the men in his brigade, who called him "the biggest little man God Almighty ever made." The Mahone era was characterized by violent rhetoric and still more violent gunplay.

Unlike their role in antebellum years, when they dealt editorially with sectionalism, slavery, states' rights, and westward expansion, the newspapers of Virginia and the men who edited and controlled them were concerned chiefly with issues of primary significance within the state itself after the close of Reconstruction. Mahone, a railroad operator, entered politics at first to safeguard his own road against the incursions of John S. Barbour and the Pennsylvania Central Railroad. Opposed by Richmond financial interests allied with Barbour through the Virginia Central Railroad, Mahone lost out. Soon, however, he emerged as leader of a movement to renegotiate the crushing burden of antebellum debt under which Virginia labored, in order to safeguard funds for the state's public school system. Conservatives favored paying the prewar debt in order to safeguard Virginia's "honor," even though to do so meant that virtually nothing would be left for education; Mahone and his fusion of Republicans and dissatisfied Democrats demanded that the debt be readjusted, on the theory that the needs of the people of the Old Dominion came first, and that the state's creditors, many of them English, should be made to participate in the loss of capital and resources that the defeat of the Confederacy had brought.

The political cleavage swiftly developed into a liberal-conservative division, with Mahone's forces favoring public education, extension of the franchise, abolition of the whipping post as a punishment for lawbreaking, increased public revenues through taxes on the valuation of property, and reduction of taxes on land that hit the farming community with special severity. As might be expected, black Virginians generally supported Mahone and the Readjusters. But Mahone's dictatorial ways and his willingness to cooperate with the national Republican party to achieve his ends soon alienated many of his supporters and allies. The Readjuster-Funder split divided Virginia politics along class lines in numerous ways, and the bitterness and rancor, allied with widespread corruption and Mahone's use of black voters as a bloc, brought to the state's politics an acrimony and viciousness such as had seldom before occurred.

Three influential Virginia editors, William E. Cameron, William C. Elam, and John Hampden Chamberlayne, were heavily involved with "Billy" Mahone. Cameron and Chamberlayne started out as his great admirers and then broke with him. Elam was with him all the way.

William Evelyn Cameron is remembered especially for his four years as governor from 1882 to 1886, but his journalistic career was a distinguished one. He edited papers in Petersburg and Norfolk, and was on the editorial staffs of two papers in Richmond. Some of his polemical editorial writings are among the most brilliant and scathing in the state's newspaper history.

A native of Petersburg, and descended from aristocratic forebears including the Scottish chieftain Ewan Lochiel, Cameron had little formal education above the academy level. As a youth he served as assistant purser on a Mississippi steamboat and became acquainted with Mark Twain, who was engaged as a pilot. Ambitious for an army career, he enrolled late in 1860 at Washington University, St. Louis, hoping to prepare himself for West Point. But with the outbreak of the Civil War he enlisted in the Confederate forces as a private. Cameron fought in all the battles of Lee's army from Seven Pines on, except Sharpsburg, and he was prevented from taking part in that sanguinary action by a severe wound sustained at Second Manassas. Joining Mahone's brigade on his recovery, he rose to assistant adjutant general, and after Appomattox continued his close association with Mahone.

Returning to Petersburg from the war, he was chosen editor of the newly established Norfolk *Virginian*. But in 1867 he went back to Petersburg and bought the Petersburg *Index*. With that paper Cameron plunged into the bitter political feuds that were rocking the state. U.S. District Judge John C. Underwood of New York had come to Virginia after Lee's surrender, and was delivering himself of some astonishing judgments concerning the people and mores of the Old Dominion. In a charge to the grand jury sitting in Norfolk on the case of Jefferson Davis, he said, for example, that the Confederacy had "burned towns and cities with a barbarity unknown to Christian countries, scattered yellow fever and smallpox among the poor and helpless, and finally struck down one of earth's noblest martyrs to freedom and humanity," namely Lincoln. Richmond's "licentiousness" was such, he declared, that "probably a majority of the births were illegitimate."

Cameron's *Index* lashed out at the judge as an "absurd, blasphemous, cowardly, devilish, empirical, fanatical, ghoulish, horrible, ignorant, jacobinical . . . Yankeeish zero." It was joined by the Richmond press, notably the *Whig,* which termed His Honor a "dirty demagogue" and "monster," an "ignorant blockhead" and an "indisputable ass."

When the so-called Underwood Constitution was adopted by a stacked convention presided over by Judge Underwood, the Petersburg *Index* termed it "that hell-born instrument," and added: "The man among us who could favor its adoption is a traitor to his manhood and an enemy to his fellow-citizens. . . . We challenge the mendacity and malignity of those who would subject Virginia to the misery of such government."

Henry H. Wells, like Underwood a New Yorker, had served as governor of Virginia immediately after the war and was running for another term in 1869 against a third New Yorker, Gilbert C. Walker. The *Index* found Walker much less odious than Wells and spared few derogatory adjectives in its references to his opponent.

"Were his political instincts as noble and generous as they are low and selfish," the paper said of Wells, "he would still be obnoxious beyond all other men. For he has played the broker upon Virginia's possessions, and would have sold her people's heritage for an agent's commission." When Wells was defeated by Walker, the *Index* exulted: "The devil is commonly credited with the paternity of lies, but the Virginia carpetbag perjurers, headed by Wells, have usurped the old man's patent, and hold special priority in the science of misrepresentation and falsehood."

Even such blistering words as these were not quite so libelous as those exchanged in the course of the Wells-Walker campaign between Cameron of the *Index* and Robert W. Hughes of the Richmond *State Journal*. Hughes was a native of Powhatan County who had been reared in Abingdon and was an old-line Republican. Later he would run for governor unsuccessfully against James L. Kemper and then be appointed judge of the U.S. District Court, succeeding Judge Underwood. Like Cameron, Hughes was a writer of exceptional gifts. The following appeared from his pen in the *State Journal* about a month before the Wells-Walker election—in support of Wells:

> If names could typify the meaning of words, the *mene mene tekel upharsin,* which a bloody and destructive history has pronounced upon the sectional party that has so long ruled and ruined in Virginia, is especially expressed in such names as Bocock, Douglas and Aylett. These are but types that have gone forth to re-invoke the people to courses of treason. It is well for the causes of loyalty, reconstruction and state regeneration that a class of parricides so notorious, with the mark of Cain on their foreheads and the guilt of Cain upon their consciences, have gone out as champions of a discontented, remonstrant and incorrigible sectionalism.... They are ready to drag down the commonwealth into a deeper damnation than that in which she already writhes and perishes.

The three men named in the editorial were evidently Thomas S. Bocock, former U.S. congressman and Speaker of the Confederate Congress; Beverley B. Douglas, state senator and congressman, and Patrick Henry Aylett, lawyer and journalist. The attack brought from Cameron's *Index* the following:

> There is one journalist in this state who is at the same

time sufficiently capable as a writer and utterly degraded enough in character to have indited these lines. He is one of those who lent truculence and almost inhuman bitterness to the Richmond *Examiner* during the war—the man upon whom John M. Daniel [editor of the *Examiner*] chiefly relied for his strongest appeals to the worst passions of our people. . . .

His first act after the war was to connect himself with the dirtiest of all the poisonous sheets which disgraced Virginia since 1864—the Richmond *Republic*—and his undeniable versatility as a writer was there employed to brand as infamous all that he had advocated for six years previous. His venal pen has been sold to the highest bidder. . . .

He is now contributing editorially to the Richmond *State Journal,* which has lost thereby four-fifths of its previous claims to respectability. The people of Virginia want no stronger evidence of unreliability in a public print than to know that the sentiments flow from the purchased pen of Robert W. Hughes.

Such insults could only result in a summons to the "field of honor." Accordingly, the principals and their seconds repaired surreptitiously to the vicinity of Chester. But before any shots could be fired, officers of the law suddenly appeared and arrested some of the would-be duelists. They were put under bond to keep the peace within the borders of Virginia. "Honor" had to be satisfied, however, and the two groups determined to meet over the border in North Carolina. They traveled to the appointed spot in passenger cars attached to a freight train. This time no constable appeared to interrupt the proceedings. When the duel began, Cameron was said to have missed deliberately, whereas Hughes's ball struck Cameron in the left side of the chest. It was not a dangerous wound. Hughes demanded a second round and Cameron agreed. But the latter's physician forbade him to continue, saying that he was in no condition to do so. That ended the matter, and all parties went back to Petersburg by a return freight train.

Years later, when Cameron was governor and Hughes was a federal judge, they happened to meet in a Richmond hotel bar. Lenoir Chambers relates what happened next in his admirable book, *Salt Water and Printer's Ink,* to which I am greatly indebted:

> Cameron walked toward Hughes, touched his arm, and said "Judge, let me buy you a drink." "That would be a pleasure," Hughes replied.
>
> Arm in arm they walked to the bar.

Cameron's rise to the governorship had been achieved with the aid of Mahone, who also had been largely responsible for his election as mayor of Petersburg. Cameron was a Conservative who backed "readjusting," or scaling down, the state debt, the principal issue on which Mahone had ridden to power. At this time, the "Hero of the Crater" had turned Republican, the party to which Judge Hughes belonged. All of this doubtless had a bearing on the development of more cordial relations between Hughes and Cameron.

Before Cameron broke with Mahone because he felt that the general was meddling in his affairs as governor, he delivered a speech in which he defended himself from aspersions in the opposition press. In the course of it Cameron declared that he "would not give the parings of General Mahone's toe-nails for all the boasted chivalry, honesty and aristocracy of all the Bourbon Funders in Virginia." (The Bourbon Funders were the bitter opponents of Mahone's and Cameron's plans for "readjusting" the state debt.) It was said thereafter that Cameron had "immortalized the toe-nails of Mahone," and the Funder press, advocating the funding, or payment in full, of the state debt, referred to him repeatedly as "the toe-nail governor."

Cameron had an enlightened view of the race problem and was sympathetic to Mahone's attitude on the issue. As editor of the Petersburg *Index,* he had expressed fury over the burning of a large, unfinished Negro church in the town. The *Index* voiced "regret and indignation that there could have been found within the limits of Petersburg one heart so profligate and abandoned to inflict this outrage on our colored people." The paper went on to urge that every possible means be taken "to hunt down the author or authors . . . and at the same time extend whatever assistance may be in our power." With respect to Negro schools, the paper said that "it is in our interest, as well as for their own, that their minds should be enlightened. . . . as a class they have conducted themselves remarkably well."

As governor, Cameron appointed blacks to the Petersburg and Richmond school boards. He also had a leading role, along with Mahone, in securing the enactment of legislation greatly increasing appropriations for schools for the blacks, in establishing the Negro Normal and Collegiate Institute (now Virginia State University) and an asylum for insane blacks (Central State Hospital), and in abolishing the whipping post as well as the poll tax that had been a prerequisite for voting. (Later, as a member of the state constitutional convention of 1901–02 Cameron would move in the opposite direction and aid in bringing about the wholesale disfranchisement of the blacks.)

Governor Cameron displaced many of the boards of state educational institutions, and improvement undoubtedly resulted in some instances, since more than one of these boards, appointed by the Funders, had become stodgy and inactive. At the Medical College of Virginia, however, the chief executive ran into an unexpected snag. When the newly appointed Board of Visitors went to the college to take over, it was met by a committee of the old board, headed by Dean James B. McCaw, which refused to be superseded, locked the doors, and had the police arrest one of the arriving delegation. The governor appealed the matter to the Virginia Supreme Court of Appeals. While awaiting the verdict of that tribunal, the pro-Cameron Richmond *Whig* published the following verses concerning Dean McCaw:

> His name is Doctor McCaw
> He's Professor of Cheek and Jaw,
> And he won't admit Visitors
> Nor other inquisitors,
> To see us cut and saw—
> Haw, haw!
> Yes, his name is Doctor McCaw,
> And he cares not a drachm for the law,
> For he's Dean of the Faculty,
> Chief Quack of the Quackalty
> And he strikes all beholders with awe
> Haw, haw!

The court held that Governor Cameron had exceeded his authority in seeking to oust the Medical College board. Its members accordingly remained at their posts.

After his term as governor, William Cameron practiced law in Petersburg for several years. In 1896 he fought against free silver, joining the Gold Democrats in their futile effort to prevent William Jennings Bryan from carrying the state. He was becoming increasingly conservative, as previously noted. Cameron became a journalist once more to close out his career. In 1906 he was chosen editor of the Norfolk *Virginian-Pilot*, forty years after he had served as editor of the Norfolk *Virginian* at age twenty-three. In addition to holding the post of editor of the Petersburg *Index* for five years immediately following the Civil War, he had been on the editorial staffs of the Richmond *Whig* and *Enquirer* in the 1870s. George W. Bagby, no mean judge, termed him in 1879 "in a certain vein, the best political writer in the state; humor and wit in a high degree."

Cameron presided over the editorial page of the *Virginian-Pilot* from 1906 to 1919, when he retired at age seventy-seven. By then his outlook was a far cry from the liberal stance he had taken years before as a close collaborator with Mahone, but few questioned his integrity or his ability. The crusade for statewide prohibition, led by the slippery but able Methodist bishop, James Cannon, Jr., was opposed by the *Virginian-Pilot,* but to no avail. The paper was wholeheartedly behind the United States and its allies in the First World War. Cameron's retirement from the editorship almost coincided with the end of that conflict. He died in 1927.

John Hampden Chamberlayne occupied editorial positions in Petersburg, Norfolk, and Richmond that almost paralleled those held by Cameron, and he too was a brilliant writer and forceful personality. Both men had good relations with "Billy" Mahone before breaking with him, but Chamberlayne broke earlier— over Mahone's "readjusting" the state debt. The louder Mahone squeaked his orders to his henchmen in that fight, the more hostile Chamberlayne became.

Ham Chamberlayne, as he was widely known, was born in Richmond. After education in the academies of that day, he enrolled at the University of Virginia, taking his M.A. in 1858 at age twenty. With the mounting intersectional tension, Chamberlayne wrote an editorial for the Richmond *Examiner* in December 1860 urging immediate action by Virginia. "Now is the day and now the hour to do; else we will be a hissing and a scorn among the nations," he declared.

With the outbreak of hostilities, Chamberlayne enlisted in the artillery and fought bravely throughout the conflict. His letters to his family from the front are among the most significant and vivid to come out of the war. He minced no words concerning men and events. Usually his comments were much to the point, but occasionally he spoke with undue harshness and without adequate information. The most conspicuous instance of this was his charge in family letters that General William N. Pendleton, his artillery commander, was guilty of "outrageous imbecility," "ridiculous incompetency," and "base cowardice."

Lieutenant Chamberlayne was repeatedly commended for bravery by his superiors, as is attested by letters from Generals Stonewall Jackson and A. P. Hill. His most spectacularly intrepid feat occurred at the Battle of the Crater. He was ill in a hospital when two officers of his battery either were seriously wounded or fled from the field (the accounts differ). Chamberlayne rushed from his sick bed to the scene of action, took command of the battery, ordered the men to their guns, and turning them upon the enemy, made an important contribution to the Confederate victory. He was promoted to captain as a result of this and other exhibitions of courage and initiative, and remained in command of the battery until its surrender at Appomattox.

Then came a period of extreme hardship for the twenty-seven-year-old former soldier in Lee's army. Penniless and without employment, he settled as a farmer in the Green Springs section of Louisa County. For eighteen months he strove to coax from the none-too-fertile soil a bare living for his mother, his brother, and himself. The strain was such that by the spring of 1867 "he suffered a complete physical and nervous breakdown," which, according to his son, the Rev. Dr. Churchill G. Chamberlayne, incapacitated him throughout a whole year for effort of any kind. "That year was the darkest of his life," Dr. Chamberlayne wrote.

By late 1868 his health had improved, and he moved to Petersburg, where he joined the staff of the *Index*. After serving as associate editor under William Cameron, he became editor when Cameron moved to the Richmond *Whig* in January, 1871. Chamberlayne occupied the editorship of the *Index* for almost three years, and was at that time a staunch supporter of Mahone. He was a delegate to the 1873 convention which met to name candidates for state offices, and was allied there with the "Hero of the Crater."

When James Barron Hope relinquished the editorship of the Norfolk *Virginian* in 1873 to become editor of the newly established Norfolk *Landmark*, the *Virginian* cast about for an accomplished successor and found him in thirty-five-year-old Ham Chamberlayne. This was quite a challenge, since, in the opinion of Lenoir Chambers, Hope's professional capacities "were not equaled by any other Virginian of his time." Captain Chamberlayne would be in direct competition with the talented and admired Hope, an accomplished and graceful writer not only of prose but of poetry as well. In this difficult situation, Chamberlayne doubtless received inspiration from his newly acquired bride, Mary Walker Gibson, daughter of the Rev. Churchill J. Gibson of Petersburg.

Shortly after taking the editorial helm at the *Virginian,* Chamberlayne paid his respects to U.S. Judge John C. Underwood, who had just died. "To speak of this event with the customary decorum is not easy," he wrote. "The public life of the dead man was marked by nothing good or upright.... his whole judicial career proved him an ignorant, a vindictive and a corrupt judge ... the first judge who had brought infamy to the bench, the first judge to earn the contempt of the state, the first to bring disgrace upon it."

The youthful editor caused a sensation in 1874 with his commencement address at Randolph-Macon College. According to one account, "For the first time in our history the mirror was held up frankly to ex-slaveholders by one of themselves—the defects of the system shown without gloss or apology, and the fatal consequences pointed out, as if the orator stood in Faneuil Hall instead of on the platform of a Southern college." The address was loudly applauded by those who heard it, and was widely copied. As good a speaker as he was a writer, Chamberlayne was in demand thereafter on many public occasions.

After two and a half years, he resigned in 1876 from the *Virginian*. He was felt to have performed well at the paper's editorial helm, but there was an opportunity in Richmond that he could not refuse. This was to become the owner and editor of the newly established Richmond *State,* a position in which he made a most distinguished record in the few years that remained to him.

Ham Chamberlayne came back to Richmond at a time when politics was heating up. He was still friendly with Mahone, but when the hundred-pound "king of the lobby," in his peg-top trousers and Prince Albert coat, began urging "readjustment" of the state debt, it was too much for Chamberlayne. Thereafter he fought Mahone with everything he had.

Things in Richmond were rather hectic in other respects too. The town was recovering slowly from the war and its aftermath, and citizens were able at last to enjoy themselves a bit. But Episcopal Bishop Francis M. Whittle was not amused by such outlandish diversions as the round dance and the waltz, and proclaimed that "this scandal is not to be tolerated." Shocked, furthermore, to find Episcopalians drinking whiskey, the bishop denounced the "dreadful and sinful habit of intemperance which appears to be on the increase." Flowers in the churches at Easter were also placed on His Grace's *index expurgatorium.*

In the fight over the state debt, Chamberlayne and his fellow Funders were embarrassed by the fact that they were Democrats, for the Northern Democrats were not to their liking. The *State* "denounced the people of the North as a 'rude,' 'uncultured' and ill-bred lot who lacked respect for the 'traditional past' and who wasted their lives in a degrading struggle for 'filthy lucre,'" as James Tice Moore paraphrased it in his work on the controversy over Virginia's debt.

Chamberlayne served in the House of Delegates as a Funder in 1879 and 1880. When the McCulloch Bill was passed in 1879, funding the debt principal at lower interest rates, the *State* said: "Unsettle the settlement [sought under the bill], attempt to readjust the readjustment already made, and you might as well put a keg of powder under the Capitol and blow it up—the effect in either case will be the same." The plan failed, nevertheless.

In the contest with the Readjusters for statewide offices in 1881, with Cameron running for governor, the *State* argued that the future of "pure white Saxon government" was at stake, with white supremacy in danger. Frank S. Blair of Wythe County, a prominent Republican, was a particular target of the *State*, which felt strongly that Virginia was honor bound to pay her debt in full. In this connection, the paper said:

"Once upon a time," as the old stories begin, there was a man named Blair. He was a lawyer and a politician and a stumper through the land. He was not well-known and never would have been well-known if he hadn't said one distinctive thing that people would not and could not forget: "Honor won't buy a breakfast."

Now every man loves his breakfast, and without his breakfast no man can be happy. But many men love their honor, and they even go so far as to love it better than breakfast. . . .

Mr. Blair might have said honor won't buy a dinner or a supper, but evidently breakfast is Mr. Blair's favorite meal. . . . Some fine morning, when he has finished one of his breakfasts, not bought with honor, and has gracefully arranged his napkin, knife and fork, he will rise from the table strengthened for the work of applying the principles, or rather the non-principles, of repudiation of the national debt. Of course the Republicans who shall have assisted him in breaking down the credit of Virginia, will not fail him when he undertakes the mightier task of breaking down the credit of the United States.

Editor Chamberlayne's determined effort to thwart the readjustment of Virginia's debt and to defeat the gubernatorial candidacy of William Cameron was futile. The debt was scaled down and Cameron was elected.

Ham Chamberlayne had strong views on many public issues, and he did not hesitate to express them. He was an unabashed elitist. "The best government in the world is the rule of the best people," he wrote. He went on to say that "all men may aspire to the highest ranks in their class, and each class may continue to improve its condition." His love of Virginia was profound and enduring. As his son expressed it: "No woman . . . held the first place in Ham Chamberlayne's heart. That place was reserved for his native state, Virginia. Though he was too clear-sighted to be blind to her faults . . . his love of Virginia was the moving passion of his life." He was convinced, furthermore, that the old commonwealth's greatest triumphs lay in the future. Five of his public addresses survive, and four of them have as their theme, "Awake, and plan and work for the greater Virginia that is to be."

Chamberlayne was also a leader in calling for reconciliation with the North. When Rutherford B. Hayes became president in 1876, the *State* led in urging acceptance of the situation, and the paper served as "a barrier and breakwater to the flood of passion that threatened to burst forth on all sides." Many backers of Samuel J. Tilden, the Democratic candidate, were convinced that the presidency had been stolen from him, but the *State* sought to persuade them that the outcome should be accepted.

Some years after the war, Chamberlayne was standing on a street corner in Petersburg when the United States flag happened to pass. A friend remarked to him that it was "a beautiful flag, " and the former Confederate officer replied: "Yes, it is the most beautiful flag in the world. I fought against it, but I love it."

Chamberlayne's career was tragically cut short when he was only forty-three and at the height of his influence and prestige. Like so many other leading Virginia editors of the nineteenth century, he died long before his work was accomplished. After a brief illness, pneumonia carried him off on February 18, 1882.

There was widespread grief at his sudden passing. The House of Delegates adjourned in his honor and attended his funeral at St. James Episcopal Church. Expressions of sorrow, accompanied by high praise, appeared in an astonishing number of newspapers, not only throughout Virginia but also along the East Coast from Charleston to Philadelphia. Some bordered their comments in black.

The Negro paper *Red Star* complimented Captain Chamberlayne as "a man of extraordinary energy, an accomplished conversationalist and one of the ablest of Virginia journalists . . . a hearty advocate for the upbuilding of his country and his state." And it went on: "Though confronting him as an enemy on all the great public battlefields of the past sixteen years, we can well say . . . that John Hampden Chamberlayne has left a name that will not soon be forgotten."

Susan D. Smedes, who was related to him, wrote in the *Memorials of a Southern Planter*:

This rarely-gifted young man had already made his influence felt throughout the state of Virginia, and he was regarded as her ablest citizen among the rising generation. The briefest notice of Hampden Chamberlayne would be incomplete without some mention of his incomparable powers as a conversationalist. Persons familiar with the most brilliant society of the Old World have declared that he would have shone preeminent and almost without a peer in London or Paris. In heart and character he was as richly endowed as in mind.

In *Belles, Beaux and Brains of the Sixties* Thomas C. DeLeon wrote: "Ham Chamberlayne had his sister's wit and humor, and was a great scholar, but eccentric and saturnine. He was a brave soldier and a true friend, a forceful, fluent writer, with a great future before him...."

Modern medicine might well have saved this illustrious editor and citizen for several more decades, but fate decreed otherwise.

The third notable editor of the Mahone era was Colonel William C. Elam, who wielded a vitriolic pen on behalf of Mahone's policies, fought duels as a result of insults hurled in the course of these wrangles, and was twice seriously wounded.

Elam was a North Carolinian and former Confederate officer who had contributed to George W. Bagby's *Southern Literary Messenger* on the eve of the Civil War. His series of sketches and stories for that publication was signed "Klutz," and Bagby paid him at the rate of "one dollar the printed page." To be paid anything at all in that era by a Southern publication was unusual, which attests to the value Bagby placed on Elam's work. In fact, the *Messenger*'s editor predicted that he would "write the best Southern novel yet." This was not to be, but the Tar Heel scribe wielded a savage quill in the violent controversies surrounding Mahone and his policies. He was an old-line Whig, and it was as editor of the Richmond *Whig* that he became a center of fierce polemics in postbellum Virginia journalism. Later he moved to the Norfolk *Pilot,* and continued his vigorous and fearless editorializing.

The collaboration between Mahone and Elam was so close that Mahone moved his headquarters to the offices of the *Whig,* which he controlled. Elam was secretary of the State Readjuster Committee as well as editor of the paper. The *Dispatch* and the *State* were his principal journalistic opponents. Under the caption "Political Pirates," the *Whig* harked back to early April, 1865, and the departure of the Confederate government from Richmond as the city was falling. "The president, governor, and the whole bomb-proof corps grabbed the remaining swag and sneaked away," said the *Whig* in 1880.

The governor in question was "Extra Billy" Smith, and his son, Colonel Thomas Smith, was infuriated. He challenged Elam and the latter accepted. They met at 6:00 A.M. on the banks of a creek behind Oakwood Cemetery, seeking to avoid the police. The antagonists stood twelve paces apart, and at the signal both fired. Elam was hit in the chin, the ball splitting the bone and lodging in the tongue. Smith was not hit. He rushed to Elam, and expressed regret at wounding him. The latter replied that he would rather receive a wound than give one. An unusually small charge of powder had been placed inadvertently in the two pistols, which saved Elam's life. Warrants were issued for both men, but Smith got away.

Elam never tired of lambasting the "Bourbons," who urged payment of the state debt in full and contended that "readjustment" meant repudiation. He was tireless in attacking "the Brokers and the Broker Press," the "Scribe and Pharisee" parsons who backed the Funders, the office-holding set who "generally train with the courthouse clique, and always believe that money and position are stronger than the people." Sometimes he misrepresented the facts outrageously, but the Funders were none too scrupulous themselves on occasion. It was an all-out, dog-eat-dog confrontation. Everything from sulphurous rhetoric to Colt revolvers was resorted to. And although Elam professed to be scornful of just about everything the Bourbons represented, he lived punctiliously by their code duello.

127

Before Elam came on the scene, Mahone had been deeply involved in a successful attempt to consolidate three railroads extending from Norfolk to Bristol. His plan was supported generally in Norfolk, the Southside, and the Southwest, while opposition centered around Richmond, Lynchburg, and the Shenandoah Valley. Both advocates and opponents were seeking to promote their own trade and business interests. The debt controversy was also involved, since the proposed sale of the state's prewar investments in these railroads had a direct bearing on payment of the debt.

The infighting in this matter was vicious. Legislation was passed in 1871 providing for the sale of Virginia's railroad investments, at a tremendous loss to the state. Also passed was a bill funding the prewar debt. Allen W. Moger writes in his authoritative book, *Virginia: Bourbonism to Byrd*:

> Students of this period substantially agree that the "legislation was procured by an unholy combination of the forces of the bankers, brokers and speculators and railroads... assisted by a few excellent men who were influenced by a desire to protect what they believed to be the essential credit and unsullied honor of the commonwealth." Some votes were bought, and many leaders most concerned about the state's honor and recovery had direct financial interests in one or both of these pieces of legislation.

Mahone, directing much of the intensive lobbying, acted through agents known as "sea turtle," "crab," and "fish." The New York *Times* reported that "in the parlors of a certain hotel there was a table on which two gigantic bowls were placed; one was filled with punch, the other contained greenbacks."

Passage of the Funding Act in 1871 was far from marking the end of the debt controversy, which would continue for years. When

Colonel Elam joined the *Whig* as editor in the late 1870s, "read-justment" was still a steaming issue. Thirty-nine leading citizens, including several clergymen, formed a committee in 1877 "to preserve the credit of the state." The *Dispatch* and the *State* hailed this Committee of Thirty-Nine, but the *Whig* blasted it. Mahone's organ even published the amount of coupons the doctors of divinity on the committee had used to pay taxes.

John Hampden Chamberlayne, as editor of the *State,* was completely uninhibited in his attacks on Mahone and his cohorts, but though always ready to accept any challenge, it somehow happened that he was not involved in a single duel during his editorial career. Richard F. Beirne, his associate who became editor after his death, was drawn into more than one "affair of honor," however. Beirne, whose language was as colorful and vitriolic as anybody's, proceeded to call H. H. Riddleberger, whose name was attached to the debt settlement, a crook. The "Gamecock of the Valley" couldn't take that lying down, and sent a challenge at once. The two men met in Hanover County near Ashland. When the word was given to fire, both pistols snapped harmlessly. To Beirne's intense embarrassment, his friends had forgotten to bring caps for the pistols. The duel was an obvious fiasco. It was so embarrassing to Beirne that he is said to have sought an opportunity to prove his courage, which he had in abundance. It came when he penned a ferocious editorial entitled "Who Are the Niggers?" In it he charged Mahone and his backers with favoring mixed marriages, mixed schools, and opposing honest white men. The real "niggers," the *State* declared, were the "Mahoneites" in general and Editor Elam in particular; and it added: "In making this comment on Boss Mahone, we wish it to be distinctly understood by all his corrupt henchmen that what we say and have said of him we mean and have meant of them personally, individually and collectively, and in any other sense they may choose to feel. A more vicious, corrupt and degraded gang never followed any adventurer than those who hang about the petty boss."

Elam, who was as fearless as Beirne, retorted next day under the heading "A Few Necessary Remarks": "Not only does the *State* lie, but its 'editor and owner' lies, and the poor creature who may have written the article in question also lies—all jointly and severally—deliberately, knowingly, maliciously and with the inevitable cowardice that is always yoked with insolent bravado." Elam went on to say that the *State*'s fierce denunciation "might alarm us, but for our recollection that the hero (the Bombastes Furioso) of the *State* has the singular reputation of having illustrated his untamed valor only by going upon the field without caps."

There could be but one outcome for this venomous exchange. Beirne, age twenty-seven, challenged Elam, age forty-seven, immediately, and the antagonists repaired to a point near Hanover Junction. The weapons would be Colt Navy revolvers, fired at eight paces to accommodate Elam's nearsightedness. But as the duel was about to begin, a police officer appeared and arrested several of the principals. Elam and Beirne were determined to have it out, however, and a week later they met near Waynesboro despite all hazards and difficulties. Both missed at the first fire, and Beirne demanded another. Elam missed again, but Beirne wounded his antagonist severely in the hip. Beirne thereupon raised his hat and left the field.

Elam was slow in recovering from his wound, but this did not inhibit his challenging Charles O. Cowardin of the *Dispatch* when they had a sharp disagreement. This time the encounter was prevented by the police. Despite his defective vision, Colonel Elam never hesitated to risk his neck with "pistols at ten paces."

The race issue was constantly at the fore in the controversies surrounding Mahone. He appealed to the blacks with educa-

Ruins of downtown Richmond, 1865. Note the women in
mourning at lower right
—*Valentine Museum*

Collapse of floor of State Capitol,
Richmond, April 27, 1870. Draw-
ing by W. L. Sheppard for
Harper's Weekly
—*Valentine Museum*

James E. Hunnicutt
—*Virginia State Library*

Judge John C. Underwood
—*Virginia State Library*

Richmond *Dispatch* building at
Twelfth and Main Streets
—*Richmond Newspapers*

General William Mahone
—*Richmond Newspapers*

Governor Charles T. O'Ferrall
—*Virginia State Library*

John Mercer Langston, Virginia's
first black Congressman
—*Richmond Newspapers*

William C. Elam

William E. Cameron
—*Virginia State Library*

J. G. (Parson) Massey
—*Virginia State Library*

John Hampden Chamberlayne
—*Virginia Historical Society*

Carter Glass, as photographed in 1920s
—*Richmond Newspapers*

John Mitchell, Jr.
—*Richmond Newspapers*

Richmond *Planet* for December 14, 1907
—*Richmond Newspapers*

Front page of Richmond *Times* for
February 16, 1898
—*Richmond Newspapers*

Richmond *Times* building at
Tenth and Bank Streets
—*Richmond Newspapers*

Statue of Joseph Bryan in Monroe Park, Richmond
—Richmond Newspapers

tional and penal programs that were badly needed, and they usually supported him overwhelmingly. Mahone's critics stressed the race issue excessively, and exaggerated what he was doing for the blacks. There was demagoguery on both sides. The *Whig* declared in 1881 that Negroes were in the majority in more than one-third of Virginia's counties, but that the Negroes and Republicans were placing whites in county offices, often white Conservatives. In fact, the "Negro rule" which Mahone's enemies claimed he was seeking to impose was not even approached except in a very few localities, and certainly not in the state as a whole. The city councils of Petersburg and Danville were briefly controlled by blacks, but the results were not alarming. Blacks were given a few minor state jobs, but nothing of major importance. When John Mercer Langston, a black, ran successfully for Congress from Southside, Virginia, Mahone opposed him, on the ground that in his opinion the time had not come for a Negro to serve in Congress from Virginia.

The *Whig* said in 1883: "All citizens, whether white or otherwise, have the equal right under the laws . . . to vote and be voted for, and to be appointed to any political office. . . . But when it comes to a question of sociology, men will hold their own prejudices . . . and decide such questions for themselves, according to the spirit and taste of the age and community in which they live." Four years later the *Whig* declared that whites would never tolerate mixed schools and would abolish the public schools first. The paper asserted that it represented "the original, independent thinkers who constitute the masculine-minded men in these steam-power times."

Former governor Henry A. Wise was a surprising recruit to the Readjuster cause; he referred to the Conservatives as "dirt-eating male bawds." A force for good in several directions and a man of ability, Wise had his eccentricities. After the war, for example, he "gardened furiously while wearing a frock coat and black top hat, and sometimes even carrying an umbrella," his biographer, Craig Simpson says. He frequently wore this same garb on his daily trips to market, while spewing tobacco juice.

For several years, Mahone was riding high, with the aid of Elam's *Whig*. He was U.S. senator from Virginia and in control of the state's politics. But after Fitzhugh Lee was elected governor in 1885, succeeding Mahone's man Cameron, the whole Readjuster coterie lost power steadily. Important leaders who had been closely allied with Mahone broke with him. The list included John S. Wise, who had been his unsuccessful candidate for governor against Fitz Lee; "Parson" Massey, an extremely able Baptist clergyman whose bid for the governorship had been thwarted by Mahone in 1881; and Cameron. These men were alienated by Mahone's arrogance and his dictatorial propensities. His ruthless and high-handed methods included requiring a pledge from each of his appointees to "vote for all measures, nominees and candidates . . . as the caucus may agree upon." Furthermore, each officeholder was compelled to contribute a percentage of his or her salary to the Readjuster "war chest"—five per cent for state employees living in Richmond and two per cent for federal employees.

John S. Wise was so embittered by all this that he remarked, "The only way Mahone will bury the hatchet is in the head of everyone who opposes him." "Parson" Massey, who was elected lieutenant governor with Fitzhugh Lee and who had become a key figure in frustrating some of Mahone's schemes in the General Assembly, had served previously as a major Mahone lieutenant. When he was prevented by Mahone from obtaining the gubernatorial nomination, the *Whig* praised him highly for the manner in which he accepted this disappointment. The paper referred to his "graceful and patriotic course," and added, "Service so great as his, abilities so various and conspicuous, associated with so magnanimous a temper, will never be forgotten." But after Massey joined the opposition, the *Whig* tore into him as "that miserable old political tramp."

Massey had run unsuccessfully in 1882 as a Funder for congressman-at-large against John S. Wise. Apropos of his defeat, the Mahoneites produced the following:

> Down midst de Funders
> Hear dat mournful sound!
> All de Funders am a-weeping
> Poor Massey's in de cold, cold ground.

Despite his fading fortunes, Mahone determined to make a try for the governorship himself in 1889. The *Whig* got into the act with both feet, and Elam produced a campaign pamphlet rehearsing what he said were the accomplishments for Virginia under Mahone's leadership. After listing some truly substantial achievements, Elam went on to declare that "Mahone rule" from 1879 to 1884 was "a calamity for the rascals who were turned out" but "a blessing to the state and her people." As a member of the U.S. Senate, Mahone labored on behalf of the people of Virginia "with a solicitude and success never paralleled by any of his predecessors." Mahone had turned Republican when he entered the U.S. Senate, and thereby gave that party a crucial majority of one in the upper branch of the national legislature. This quite naturally endeared him to the GOP and to Republican President Chester A. Arthur, and he was given important committee assignments and special favors for Virginia. The Funders, on the other hand, branded him "a traitor to his state, his section and his party."

Elam's campaign pamphlet charged, by contrast, that the rule of the Bourbon Democrats in Virginia had been characterized by extravagance, mismanagement, fraud, corruption, increased taxation, partisan legislation, and grievous neglect of the public schools.

In their determination to defeat Mahone once and for all, the Funders pulled out all the stops. They nominated Philip W. McKinney of Farmville, and he was fervently backed by such former Mahoneites as John S. Wise and William E. Cameron. The latter declared that "the politicians known as Mahoneites . . . are only acquainted with three elements of management—force, fraud and finance."

The Funders did not scruple to attack Mahone's war record. Although the rank of major general was conferred on the physically unimpressive soldier by General Robert E. Lee on the field of battle, immediately following the heroic performance of Mahone's brigade in the Battle of the Crater, Mahone's second in command, General D. H. Weisiger, was caustic in his comments in later years. This material was grist for the Funder campaign. Weisiger said that he was shot through the body at the Crater, "and was carried back to the covered way where Mahone was," William L. Royall related in his memoirs, on the basis of numerous conversations with Weisiger. Weisiger quoted Mahone as saying, "Weisiger, why in the hell are you and old Joe Johnston always getting yourselves shot?" Weisiger said he thought, in view of his severe wound, that it was all over with him, and he was therefore a bit indifferent about insubordination. Hence he answered, "General Mahone, if you would go where General Johnston and I go, you would get shot sometimes too." Weisiger also told Royall that he never saw Mahone under fire, and that Mahone never commanded the brigade in a single action. He added that "possibly I am not doing Mahone justice because I hated him, and he is the only man I ever hated." Confederate General Jubal A. Early, who seldom held a moderate view about anything or anybody, wrote Jefferson Davis in 1881 that Mahone was "a Contemptible coward, and was so in the war." The latter's postbellum political activities could well have colored Early's view.

The fact remains that hardly anybody but Weisiger and Early

seems to have contended seriously that Mahone was lacking in courage. General Lee's high opinion of him is echoed by Douglas Southall Freeman, who said he knew "how to fight," and his men became "the most renowned shock troops in the army." But in the political donnybrooks of the late nineteenth century, almost anything went, and below-the-belt attacks were resorted to with ritualistic regularity. After both sides had heaved mud to their heart's content, the heroic efforts of Elam and others to elect Mahone governor proved to be completely unsuccessful. McKinney won by a landslide and Mahone's political career was ended. He died six years later.

Colonel Elam left the *Whig* and founded a Republican paper in Harrisonburg. Then he served as a correspondent for the New York *Times* in Cuba. In 1895, aged fifty-nine, he became editor of the Norfolk *Pilot,* which had just passed through a stormy period under the editorship of the Rev. Sam Small, a fiery evangelist and prohibitionist. Small was a pugnacious individual who "stirred up the animals" and even engaged in fistfights. He ran the *Pilot* into the ground, getting it into libel suits and wrecking it financially. One of the libel actions was filed by "Parson" Massey, who collected damages for a sizzling attack on him in the *Pilot.* Headed "Money By the Bundle," the article was afterwards found to have been written by Richard E. Byrd, legal representative for Ginn and Company publishers, and father of Harry F. Byrd, later U.S. senator from Virginia. It alleged, in effect, that Massey, as state superintendent of public instruction, had accepted large amounts of graft from the American Book Company in connection with contracts for school textbooks. Ginn and Company had been an unsuccessful bidder on these contracts.

The trial of the case was sensational. Massey was attacked in furious fashion by John S. Wise, chief counsel for the defendant *Pilot,* and like the Rev. Sam Small a longtime enemy of Massey. In the words of the Norfolk *Virginian,* it was a "CYCLONE OF

VITUPERATION." "Never in the courts of Norfolk has there been a severer denunciation of any man," said the paper. "Massey was compared to all that was low and vile." He was "a dirty worm," Wise shouted. "I don't like him. I think he ought to have been in the penitentiary long ago." And he yelled in Massey's face, "You are dirty from your head to your feet!" But all this invective availed nothing. Massey, who sued for $50,000, won a verdict of $1,600 from the *Pilot*. It wasn't much, but it seemed to vindicate Massey. It was also another blow to the reeling *Pilot*.

This was a particularly harsh blow because the *Pilot* had just lost another libel suit involving charges it had recklessly published concerning the wife of a Baptist minister on the Eastern Shore. Without verification, it had put on the front page, with the specific approval of Sam Small, allegations that the minister had caught his wife in bed with another man. The uproar in and around Onancock, where the event was supposed to have occurred, can be imagined. The minister and his spouse sued and got $1,000 for damages. On its last legs by then, the *Pilot* couldn't pay either this amount or the $1,600 awarded Massey. The Rev. Sam Small departed, and the bankrupt paper was reorganized under new ownership, with Albert H. Granby as publisher and Colonel Elam as editor.

Elam's erstwhile ally and subsequent enemy, William E. Cameron, had written in the Norfolk *Landmark,* before it was known that Elam was coming to edit the *Pilot,* that he had "no superior on this continent as a fertile, forceful and fearless writer." Cameron stated further, "I have known him to produce three columns of matter a day for months at a time on subjects requiring accuracy of knowledge, yet never lapsing into slovenliness of style nor lacking the tenacity of his grip."

The former editorial chief of the Richmond *Whig* faced issues in Norfolk that were different from those he had dealt with in Richmond, but he was equally bellicose in addressing them. The paper remained, for a brief period, in favor of prohibition, but this did not last.

What engaged the attention of Editor Elam above all else was municipal corruption. He fumed over the failure of the authorities to punish one Ed Miars, a Democratic politician who operated a saloon, and whose plug-uglies beat up policemen when they probed his law violations. A mission school teacher who testified against Miars before the grand jury was encountered by Miars shortly thereafter on a ferry wharf. Miars walked up to him and knocked him unconscious with a blow to the jaw. The *Pilot,* whose news and editorial columns were controlled by Elam, published in its news columns the following:

Edward B. Miars, the notorious thug, cowardly ruffian, big brute, boisterous bully, dangerous desperado, tough dive keeper, low rum seller, ex-monkey house man, evil doer, terror of society, and defier of all law and order, is behind prison bars in Portsmouth jail, where he was committed yesterday . . . for ten days to await the result of his latest victim's injuries.

Under the caption "A Reign of Terror," the *Pilot* said editorially:

The worst feature of the matter is the aid and comfort that are openly and outrageously extended (under cover of law) to Miars and his gang and his allied bullies by the authorities of Norfolk County, including magistrates, grand jurors and the county court, all of these actively, unblushingly and zealously acting together to deliver Miars (especially) from the just grasp of the authorities of Norfolk—not that these county officers may themselves punish Miars, but that they may shield and deliver him, and keep him at large as a terror of all law-abiding people, and all who would put down lawless

137

disorder.... As a certain kind of dogs are kept and bred for their ferocity, so these brutal roughs are kept, bred and encouraged by certain persons for special use in campaigns and elections.

The foregoing got Elam a $50 fine for contempt. He put up a terrific battle, but was unable to avoid the fine. Miars, by contrast, was not convicted of any of the charges against him, including the assault on the teacher.

Feisty as ever, Elam kept right on denouncing the Norfolk County authorities for their failure to hang anything on Miars. "There were no witnesses against him because the reign of terror still exists," said the *Pilot*. "Quiet ladies and gentlemen who saw Miars attack Morgan [the teacher] were afraid to testify against Miars.... A diligent court could have learned who those witnesses were and compelled their attendance. But so it goes. The man who created the reign of terror goes scot free.... The editor who sought to have an end put to the reign of terror is fined for contempt."

Concerning the municipal election that followed shortly thereafter, the *Pilot* asked: "Shall Norfolk fall back into the dark age of ring control, when everywhere the cities and the people are rising in their might against the old party hacks, heelers and hustlers?" The results of the election were not reassuring. Although the Democrats were swept back into office, as urged by the *Pilot*'s three rival papers, crime was soon rampant again in the city. In fact, the New York publication, *Town Topics,* termed it "the wickedest city in the country."

The Norfolk *Public Ledger* took occasion to castigate the *Pilot* for its lack of enthusiasm for certain happenings and attitudes in the city: "It may deceive the people for a while by reckless assertions and irresponsible attacks... but in a well-balanced community it will have only a brief season in which to indulge in these malicious, undignified and unprofessional attacks."

To which Elam retorted in the *Pilot*: "If our circulation is large and increasing, we cannot help it if that fact endangers the circulation and advertising patronage of the *Ledger*. We have imitated it in nothing, followed it in nothing, and now scorn the example, the mean and sordid self-seeking example, it has set in its malicious, undignified and unprofessional flings at us."

Under its new ownership and editorship, the *Pilot* was indeed showing its heels to the *Ledger* and the *Landmark,* and giving the well-established *Virginian* a hard run for its money. All this culminated in early 1899 in the merger of the *Virginian* and the *Pilot* as the *Virginian-Pilot,* with Elam as editor. Later in the year the paper claimed more circulation than all other Norfolk papers combined. But Colonel Elam was not to enjoy his editorship of the *Virginian-Pilot* for long. Heart attacks had taken their toll, and he had never been robust. He died in early 1900 at age sixty-four.

A man of exceptional talent and remarkable physical bravery, William C. Elam left his imprint on the age in which he lived. If he was unscrupulous at times, the opposition was not averse to using similar methods occasionally in the bitter infighting that characterized the era.

The journalism of that era was notable for the active participation of at least three remarkable men—William C. Elam, William E. Cameron, and John Hampden Chamberlayne. Their activities revolved to a large degree around the pint-sized figure of imperious, dictatorial, squeaky-voiced William Mahone, who set his imprint, for better or worse, on the age. Each of these editors demonstrated extraordinary capacity, and each of them influenced the course of events significantly. They should be remembered.

CHAPTER SEVEN

JOHN MITCHELL, JR., OF THE *PLANET*

J ohn Mitchell, Jr., the son of slave parents, was one of the most courageous editors and incisive writers of his time. In an era when blacks were being brutally lynched with alarming frequency, Mitchell was not afraid to speak out publicly in denunciation of these barbarities, although in so doing he risked being a victim himself. He was also scathing in his editorial references to the Confederacy at a time when the heroes of the sixties were being honored and memorialized.

In the years immediately following the end of Reconstruction, black Virginians were for the first time deeply involved in state politics. Since as might be expected they tended to vote solidly with and for those elements of the white electorate that favored the interests with which they were most concerned—better schools, support for the agricultural economy, expansion of the franchise, protection against the Klan, and abolition of the whipping post as punishment for minor crimes—their role in politics was deeply resented by many whites, the more so because the illiteracy that was widespread among blacks meant that their vote could be bought and manipulated. With the defeat of Mahone and the Republican party's loss of influence in the state, there was growing sentiment among Democrats to end the corruption and vote buying that had marred Virginia politics.

Moreover, much of Mahone's support had come from the "plain folk"—rural white small farmers and lower-middle- and working-class whites who had until the 1870s played little role in Virginia politics. Just as in all other Southern states during the 1880s and 1890s, the emergence of these voters both democratized state government and, once accommodation had been reached on matters of public education and taxation, also served to introduce a strident antiblack tone into politics. For, however much these voters had been willing to go along on a fusion ticket to achieve their goals, implicitly they were strongly antiblack in sentiment, and once the Democratic party began making its electoral appeal in terms of the maintenance of white supremacy, it was able to win their support. During the 1890s and early 1900s, therefore, almost every Southern state held a constitutional convention in which, in the name of "pure government" and an end to electoral fraud and vote buying, blacks were disfranchised and stringent Jim Crow legislation was enacted.

Black leaders like Mitchell in Virginia, who had generally supported fusion with Populist and Republican factions so long as black voters were importantly involved in state politics, realized that their interests would be best served now by an alliance, on however disadvantaged terms, with the "old" leadership within the business and financial community. By disposition and because of better education, this group tended to disapprove of the crude demagoguery and antiblack violence of many lower-class whites. The "better elements" of the white population, including many of the old antebellum aristocracy, might believe strongly in white superiority, but they were not usually personally hostile to blacks, were seldom in direct economic competition with them for jobs, and did not automatically oppose funds for black schools and colleges. As H. L. Mencken with customary hyperbole wrote of the latter-day descendant of the old Southern aristocracy vis-à-vis the "grandsons of his father's tenants, " he is "unable to share their fierce jealousy of the emerging black—the cornerstone of all their public thinking."

John Mitchell, Jr., was born in 1863 at "Laburnum, " the Henrico County estate of James Lyons, a prominent and well-to-do lawyer. Lyons was a member of the Virginia Senate, the state constitutional convention of 1850–51, and the Confederate Congress. He entertained many celebrities at "Laburnum" before the war—including Clay, Webster, and Thackeray—while during the war Jefferson Davis was a frequent guest. In 1864 the mansion was completely destroyed by fire, apparently set by a slave. Lyons erected a small cottage on the site, and after the war moved to the Stanard residence at Sixth and Grace Streets, later the Westmoreland Club.

Young Mitchell grew up amid these surroundings, and as a small boy moved on the fringes of this elite society. He served as carriage boy, driving Lyons to and from his law office. Lyons was an aristocrat who was said to be the handsomest man of his day. He did not believe that carriage boys should be educated, but he reckoned without John's mother. Rebecca Mitchell had managed to learn to read and write, despite laws forbidding the teaching of slaves, and she was determined that her bright son should have adequate schooling. So after the war, young Mitchell enrolled in the Richmond Normal and High School, founded by the Freedmen's Bureau, the agency set up by the conquering Northerners to provide schooling for the former slaves. This institution was of excellent caliber, with a nine-month term, whereas neither the black nor the white public schools that opened in 1870 had anything remotely comparable.

Mitchell revealed remarkable aptitude in his studies. He was an unusually able writer, and at the same time demonstrated exceptional artistic talent. At his graduation in 1881 at age seventeen, he was first in his class and its valedictorian, winning gold medals for scholarship, debating, and art.

College seemed out of the question for him, however; he taught school in Fredericksburg for two years and then for a year in Richmond. He began his journalistic career at that time by writing for the New York *Globe,* a Negro paper.

The Richmond *Planet* was founded in 1883 by blacks, and was openly sympathetic to General William Mahone and his Readjusters. When the Readjuster movement suffered a smashing defeat in the 1883 elections, Mitchell and nine other public school teachers who had been active in the founding of the *Planet* were fired by the city school board, in accordance with the customary functioning of the spoils system. Mitchell landed on his feet, however, for the editor of the *Planet* resigned, and he took over the editorship at age twenty-one. He would remain in the post for forty-five years.

The youthful editor lost little time in belaboring the whites of the community and state for their obvious bias against blacks and their reluctance to change. As Ann F. Alexander writes in her remarkably informative and complete Ph.D. dissertation on Mitchell (Duke University, 1973): "From the beginning Mitchell was a crusading journalist, vehement in his denunciation of the caste system of the South.... [He had] a quick intelligence, a ready wit, and a refreshing disregard for the conventions of the time."

The *Planet*'s editor was particularly incensed by the frequent lynchings that were taking place both inside and outside Virginia. He devoted more crusading zeal to fighting lynching than to any other single cause, and gained a national reputation in the process. In doing so he helped correct the slanted accounts in much of the white press, while at the same time exhibiting a lack of objectivity that, given the circumstances, is understandable.

Mitchell had a desperate struggle in his early years to keep the paper alive. He had to dun subscribers relentlessly and personally to make them pay their bills, and apparently he had to take other jobs to support himself. To make the paper profitable, it was necessary to get a circulation of 5,000, and this was a long time in coming. By the mid-1890s, however, the editor was able to announce a figure of 6,400, and the paper was solvent. A certain amount of financial support seems to have been provided in the 1880s by the Republican party. Mitchell wrote years later that it was proper for "Afro-American journalists to receive money from the Republican campaign manager, as long as it did not bring with it a sacrifice of principle." Funds from various black fraternal orders in payment for documents published by the *Planet* press also helped.

Mitchell had barely gotten his editorial seat warm when a black named Richard Walker was lynched in Prince Edward County. The *Planet* denounced the crime, whereupon an unsigned letter arrived from Prince Edward County, containing a piece of hempen rope and threatening, "If you poke that infernal head of yours in this county long enough for us to do it, we will hang you higher then he was hung." Undeterred by this menacing assertion, the twenty-two-year-old editor blasted the lynchers again in the *Planet*, saying, in the words of Shakespeare: "There are no terrors Cassius in your threats, for I am armed so strong in honesty that they pass me by like idle winds, which I respect not." Mitchell thereupon bravely, even recklessly, strapped a couple of Smith & Wesson revolvers to his person and set out for Prince Edward. He was arrested soon after his arrival and thrown into jail for a few hours, but was released unharmed.

All this caused observers in other parts of the country to take note of the presence in Richmond of a black newspaperman who was fearless, and willing to confront the white establishment in ways that were unconventional, to put it mildly. He was described as an editor who "would walk into the jaws of death to serve his race." The New York *World* termed him "one of the most daring and vigorous Negro editors . . . courageous almost to a fault."

"The best remedy for a lyncher or a cursed midnight rider," said the *Planet*, "is a 16-shot Winchester rifle in the hands of a Negro with nerve enough to pull the trigger." The paper also observed that every white mob should be compelled to "carry back one or more of the members as a silent testimonial to the unerring aim of some Negro." The *Planet* was outraged when an innocent black was lynched in Roanoke, and members of the mob were fined one dollar each and given one hour in jail. "Southern white folks have gone to roasting Negroes," Mitchell said on another occasion in his journal. "We presume the next step will be to eat them."

His reputation had spread to such a degree that he was often invited to speak in the North and West on "Southern Outrages." And at age twenty-eight he was elected president of the Afro-American Press Association, with some fifty member papers, and reelected the following two years.

Mitchell did not hesitate to attack the segregation laws—in that era an act of almost unparalleled audacity for a black man. Segregation "will not be tolerated by a free and independent people," said he. "We demand no 'social equality,'" he went on, "we insist upon our civil rights."

He assailed white men with black mistresses, adding that "Jim Crow beds are more necessary in the Southland than Jim

Crow cars. . . . White men who are so anxious to be separate from colored men must also be made to separate from colored women." He also said: "They yell about Negro supremacy and the effort of the colored man to secure social equality, and yet these same howling hypocrites live upon a plane of absolute equality with Negro women whose houses they furnish and whose illegitimate children they educate."

Racial injustices in the courts were chronicled regularly by Mitchell in his paper. A white man admitted he knifed a black man to death, but got only three months in jail and then was pardoned by the governor. A white man was fined twenty-five dollars for shooting a black man, whereas a black got five years for "threatening the life" of a white man. Many such cases were described by Mitchell.

He observed that the whites would not tolerate the "educated darkey," but would "grin and endure the shortcomings of the ignorant one." Illustrating his point he said that "a white man who twenty years ago would let Sambo off with a merciless upbraiding when he stole a chicken because he was an old slave type, illiterate and poor, will send the youthful, educated son to the penitentiary for the same offense."

Mitchell saved two Negro women in Lunenburg County from being hanged on a charge of murdering a white woman. They had been sentenced to death when he learned of the case and began an intensive campaign to save them. He raised $1,500 and employed two prominent white attorneys. They appealed the case and the charges were dropped.

Mitchell's concern with these and other obvious injustices led him to give them great emphasis in the *Planet* while downplaying more favorable developments in the area of race relations. Several commentators on his role agree that he thereby gave a distorted and unbalanced picture of events, although they unite in the conviction that he deserves all honor for his courageous attacks on unfairness in the courts and elsewhere. He urged Negroes to be thrifty and industrious, to support black businesses, to show appreciation of sympathetic and understanding whites, and to be polite to all. He repeatedly urged "race pride" upon the blacks, and proclaimed "Great is the Negro!"

It is obvious that John Mitchell is entitled to a goodly share of credit for the great strides that Richmond's blacks made when he was in his heyday. *The Negro in Virginia,* published in 1940 under the auspices of the Works Progress Administration, said: "From 1890 to 1920—when John Mitchell [Jr.] and Giles B. Jackson were acknowledged leaders in Negro fraternal, political, financial and publishing circles—Richmond was considered the most important center of Negro business activity in the world." It added that "many Negro-owned establishments successfully competed with white businesses." Among the black-owned establishments mentioned were livery stables, shoe stores, barber shops and restaurants "operated by Negroes for white patrons, " and "the most efficient laundry in the city."

Mitchell "took great delight in identifying white racists by their first names, " Ann F. Alexander writes, "while the most barbaric and repulsive white crimes received prominent first-page coverage. When a white man past his sixtieth birthday brutally raped a ten-year-old white girl, Mitchell described it as 'The Usual Crime', and made sarcastic remarks about Caucasian virtue."

He opined that "the citizen of color is not the most immoral creature on the face of the earth, " since "the white man in this, as in many other respects, is still ahead." In 1888 Mitchell wrote in the *Planet*: "The day is not far distant when a Caucasian as such will have no visible existence; for with the assimilation of the two races, superinduced by the cohabiting of white men with colored women, and *vice versa,* the proud race line will have disappeared . . . and only a God will be able to determine a true Caucasian descendant."

Addressing the whites in his newspaper on another occasion, he made the following telling comment:

> If we are ignorant, you made us so. You denied us the use of the spelling book, and lashed us if you caught us with a reader.
>
> If we are immoral, you made us so, for you used us to promote your trade in slaves, and set a premium on the fecundity of our species.
>
> If we are dishonest, you made us so, for you denied to us the necessities of life, and caused us to take that for which we had labored, and yet you called it thievery.
>
> If we are poverty-stricken, you made us so, for you denied us our wages, and for 250 years of galling slavery took for your own use the profits resulting from our toil.
>
> If we are deficient in judgment, you caused it, for . . . you undertook the job of thinking for us.

It was apparently because of his desire to upgrade the Negro's achievements in society that Mitchell praised "Justice John" Crutchfield, the eccentric Richmond police court justice. Crutchfield invariably addressed blacks as "niggers," and was in various other respects not the type that John Mitchell would be expected to admire. Yet the *Planet* praised his performance on the bench, seemingly on the theory that he was elevating the race by punishing its evildoers, even though these punishments were often erratic in the extreme. Giles B. Jackson, the city's leading black lawyer, probably for similar reasons, presented the justice with a handsome silver service on his sixty-eighth birthday, on behalf of prominent black citizens.

Jackson Ward, where Mitchell lived, one of the city's six wards, was overwhelmingly black. The youthful editor ran for city council in 1888 from the ward, and was one of seven black Republicans who won seats. Since there were forty-eight members on the council, and the blacks never had more than eight, they could always be outvoted. Several weeks after his election, Mitchell went to the Republican National Convention in Chicago as a delegate. He took no discernible part in the proceedings.

He served on the council until 1896, when he was defeated for reelection. Elections in Richmond in that era were shot through with fraud, and this played a part in Mitchell's defeat, although he had aroused animosities in the black community. He protested the "outrageous robbery," saying: "If the time has come that we must be placed in jail for demanding our rights and insisting upon our constitutional privileges, the sooner we get there, the better."

The Democrats were the chief culprits in the fraudulent methods employed. Blacks, who backed the Republicans almost unanimously, were kept from voting by the hundreds through such devices as asking them interminable and often idiotic questions at the polls. Many were illiterate and easily duped. Although many blacks got in line the night before in order to vote, hundreds were left standing more than once in front of the voting booths when the polls closed. The Anderson-McCormick law passed in 1884 and the Walton law adopted a decade later put the Democrats in firm control of the election machinery, which was designed to disfranchise black voters. Mitchell observed caustically that the Negro had been kept from voting for more than ten years, and if anybody could do any more disfranchising, or "make a dead man any 'deader' after he is dead, then the country will look with interest upon this experiment."

The unveiling of the equestrian monument to Robert E. Lee at Richmond in 1890 brought bitter comments from Mitchell and the *Planet*. As a member of the city council he expressed vehe-

ment opposition to the appropriation of $10,000 toward the cere-
mony's expenses. And in the *Planet* the whole plan to memorial-
ize Lee and the Confederacy received his scorn and derision.
With thousands of Confederate veterans from all over the South
in Richmond for the occasion, including fifty generals, the paper
sneered at the entire proceeding and questioned the courage of
those who had fought for the South in the sixties.

"The men who talk most about the valor of Lee and the blood of
the brave dead are those who never smelt powder," the newspaper
growled. "Most of them were at a table, either on top or under it,
when the war was going on." The paper added on the day of the
unveiling that the ceremonies "handed down a legacy of treason
and blood" to future generations, and provided evidence that "the
loyalty so often expressed penetrates no deeper than the surface."
It speaks well for the citizenry of Richmond that such sentiments,
and others expressed by Mitchell that were equally shocking and
outrageous in the minds of nearly all white Virginians in that
era, should have resulted in no physical harm to the editor who
voiced them. Indeed, if he received any serious threats from the
city's inhabitants, no record of them is extant. When it is remembered that this was a violent era, when gunplay, lynchings, and
threats were all too common, the restraint exhibited by Rich-
monders was remarkable. The unveiling of the Lee statue went
off without a hitch, and if the participants knew of the *Planet*'s
snarling comments, they gave no evidence of the fact.

An idea of the wide readership enjoyed by the *Planet* at this
time may be gathered from the results of a poll held by the paper
in 1891 to choose the "most popular preacher." No fewer than 393
replies came from Boston, 220 from Vicksburg, and 48 from Bir-
mingham. Evidence of the paper's international standing is apparent in the statement of Albion W. Tourgée, the Northern-born
novelist and Reconstruction judge in North Carolina who advocated civil rights: "From what I hear from the friends of liberty

in England, I think the *Planet* is better known there than any paper edited by a colored man in this country."

The *Planet*, nevertheless, went into receivership in 1892 and was offered for sale at public auction. This was brought about by suits filed against Mitchell by former associates in the *Planet* who claimed a share of the profits, such as they were. Personal rivalries in the black community were also a factor. These were fueled by the breakup of the Republican party locally into factions, with Mitchell on one side and his rivals on the other. He managed somehow to wriggle out of the disturbing situation by buying the paper back for $1,625.

As a member of the city council, Mitchell was zealous in attempting to protect the blacks from discrimination of all sorts. For example, the council decreed that buildings more than three stories high must have iron fire escapes, and the fire department committee was given increased power over the approval of building permits. Mitchell was in opposition, since the blacks had only two of the seven committee members; he feared that Negroes might not be able to meet the requirements, and that discrimination might be shown in favor of white realtors and contractors. Mitchell also fought the police department bill of 1888, since the force included no black patrolmen.

In 1895 Mitchell was a participant, with another black, in an unprecedented luncheon with the governor in the mansion. A delegation from the Massachusetts legislature had written Governor O'Ferrall that they would be visiting Richmond, and the chief executive invited them to lunch. When they arrived in the city, it was found that the delegation included a black legislator, Robert Teamoh. Whether Governor O'Ferrall knew of Teamoh's presence when he extended the invitation to lunch is uncertain. At all events he asked Mitchell to join the group, and the governor of Virginia lunched with two blacks—six years before President Theodore Roosevelt's similar luncheon at the White House with

Booker T. Washington brought a storm of criticism upon the president, from Virginia and the rest of the South.

There was considerable adverse comment on the Richmond luncheon in the *Times* and *Dispatch,* both of which assailed the governor. The *Dispatch,* as usual the more caustic of the two, attacked "the meanness, treachery and ingratitude displayed by Teamoh and Mitchell in presenting themselves at the governor's lunchtable." Demagogic Tom Watson of Georgia reached the height of absurdity by blasting O'Ferrall for sitting at table with John Mitchell "just as natural as if he was a human being." The *Planet,* by contrast, was loud in praise of the governor—whose views on the race question were, indeed, more open-minded than those of many public figures in that era.

In that same year, Booker T. Washington made his much-discussed speech at the Atlanta exposition, in which he pronounced social equality "the extremist folly," and counseled his fellow blacks, "In all things that are purely social we can be as separate as the fingers, yet as the hand in all things essential to mutual progress." The speaker urged Negroes to remain in the South and to concentrate on getting an industrial education. John Mitchell refrained from criticism of Booker Washington for his statements on the race question. He termed the address "a magnificent effort," although he disagreed with its cautious, conservative approach.

Race relations in Virginia were deteriorating steadily in the late nineties when an event at Murphy's Hotel in Richmond seemed to indicate, at least temporarily, that those relations were improving. John L. Sullivan, former heavyweight champion of the world, was having breakfast in the hotel when he began abusing William Miller, his black waiter. Sullivan was partially or completely drunk much of the time during those years, and he shouted at Miller that he had "killed two coons the night before" and that Miller would be next. Thereupon the waiter hurled a pot of hot coffee in the heavyweight champion's face, knocking him cold.

The hotel management was aghast and urged Miller to leave town at once, which he did. When he returned, however, he found himself acclaimed as a hero; more than $3,000 had poured in from admirers. William L. ("Buck") Royall, chief editorial writer for the Richmond *Times,* presented him with a silver coffee pot, inscribed "To the World's Champion Coffee Pot Fighter." Miller took his $3,000 and opened Miller's Hotel for blacks. It operated for many years.

This gratifying event was obviously not enough to stop the prevailing trend in opposition to fairer treatment of the blacks. Mitchell was becoming increasingly discouraged over the unfavorable posture of race relations. His pessimism began in 1888, when William Mahone opposed the candidacy of Negro John Mercer Langston for Congress. Mahone stated that he didn't think the time had come for a black to represent a Virginia district in the national legislature. Langston was elected anyway. Then Mahone ran for governor the following year, doing his best to disassociate himself from the blacks, and was badly defeated. The career of Mitchell's onetime ally was at an end. Then came the U.S. Supreme Court's *Plessy v. Ferguson* ruling in 1896 that public school segregation was constitutional. On top of all this, the Republican party in Virginia, to which Mitchell had looked for assistance in his crusade, evidenced indifference toward the achievement of Negro rights, and began boasting that it was "lily-white."

The state constitutional convention of 1901–02 convened in order to put into effect drastic restrictions on the franchise. Mitchell was outraged. He said that delegates to the convention stood on every street corner shouting "Nigger! Nigger! Nigger!" When the new constitution became effective, black registration in Richmond plunged from 6,427 to 760.

Whereas Jim Crow laws had been virtually nonexistent in Virginia in the 1880s, this situation began changing in the decade following. The General Assembly enacted legislation in 1900 requiring segregation on railway cars, and four years later it passed a law authorizing, but not requiring, segregation on streetcars. The Virginia Passenger and Power Company, which operated Richmond's streetcars, promptly ruled that blacks must sit in the rear.

Mitchell raged that "no act since the close of the Civil War has tended to arouse a more bitter antagonism." He addressed a mass meeting of blacks the night before the new edict went into effect, and urged them not to patronize the cars. Many took his advice and walked to and from work. "Fish salt" and witch hazel for sore feet were said to be much in demand. But the streetcar company refused to withdraw its rule, and the boycott finally collapsed. Two years later, in 1906, the General Assembly passed a law requiring blacks to sit in the rear of the streetcars. John Mitchell refused thereafter ever to ride in them. On one occasion when he arrived at the railroad station without transportation to his home, he walked the sixteen blocks carrying his luggage.

A turning point in Mitchell's career came in 1902 when he founded the Mechanics Savings Bank. The largest depositor was a fraternal order, the Knights of Pythias, of which he was an officer. Mitchell remained as editor and publisher of the *Planet*, but the deteriorating interracial situation left him badly disillusioned, and he concluded that acquiescence in the situation, advancement in the business community, and cooperation with the white leadership would be more productive than militant protest. His prominent role in the abortive streetcar strike represented a temporary departure from this approach, but thereafter his blasts against racial injustice were muted. By contrast, he embarked on a course designed to conciliate the well-to-do whites.

Astonishingly, he appealed to the white aristocracy in language hardly consistent with his previous expressions, denouncing the "poor whites of the South . . . members of the cornstalk, hog-eating class . . . who never had a Negro nurse or enjoyed the luxuries of the slaveowner."

Mitchell was especially conciliatory, even obsequious, in his relations with the banking community. He joined the American Bankers Association in 1904, the only black member, and attended the association's convention at the Waldorf-Astoria in New York. During the course of the proceedings a banker from Atlanta said something to which Mitchell took strong exception. He rushed to the front of the hall and spoke without notes for half an hour. In doing so he provided a corrective to the slanted accounts in much of the white press. If his own accounts were not always objective either, that was scarcely to be expected under the circumstances. The New York *Times* quoted Mitchell as saying: "I love the white man. There is no quarrel between me and him. . . . I am proud of the South. . . . Nowhere in the domain of finance have I found the white man other than ready to help us upward. . . . There is no fight between the intelligent white man and the intelligent Negro." The *Times* said that "the bankers rose and cheered, the women in the galleries clapped their hands and waved handkerchiefs, and dozens of the delegates rushed back toward the Negro banker, crowding around him, shaking his hand and complimenting him on his address."

Mitchell attended the meetings of the American Bankers Association annually thereafter, and served as Virginia vice-president of the organization's savings and loan division. Describing his movements on these occasions he wrote, "We moved among those white gentlemen and ladies with the same studied courtesy for which we have always been noted." Pointing out that he was sometimes stared at, he said the stares "were embarrassing even to a person of our nerve and caliber."

During these years Mitchell continually emphasized to other blacks the importance of racial pride and of launching enterprises on their own. He urged that they exhibit independence and develop the ability to achieve success through individual effort. The coming of Jim Crow and disfranchisement made this course necessary, he contended.

The president of the Mechanics Bank occupied a tastefully furnished office in the bank's five-story building at Third and Clay Streets. He was a dapper dresser, customarily wearing a "jim-swinger" long-tailed coat, striped trousers, a "gates-ajar" collar and diamond stickpin. He drove a Stanley Steamer automobile. Mitchell never married and had few, if any, close friends. His nephew described him as an intensely private person "who ate dinner alone, walked alone and bowed to no man."

In the campaign for governor of Virginia in 1921, the Republican candidate, Henry W. Anderson, and his party cohorts kept emphasizing that the GOP in the Old Dominion was "lily-white." This so infuriated the blacks that they bolted and nominated their own "lily-black" ticket. Mitchell was the nominee for governor. P. B. Young, editor and publisher of the Norfolk *Journal and Guide,* a rival Negro newspaper, refused the nomination for lieutenant governor. He termed the lily-black ticket ill-timed and unwise. Young was unhappy because he felt that the black candidates had drawn a color line by excluding whites from their party plans. In the *Journal and Guide* for October 8, 1921, he also assailed Mitchell as an inactive candidate, "rusticating in California while the other candidates for governor are stumping the state day and night for their respective tickets." Mitchell, it was pointed out in his defense, was attending the American Bankers Association convention in Los Angeles.

He was back in Virginia when a political rally was held by the blacks on October 16 in Portsmouth. Antagonism between the two factions erupted in the hall. P. B. Young sought to defend himself from allegations that he had been disloyal in criticizing the lily-black ticket. The chairman of the meeting tried to make him sit down, but he refused. Mitchell and others then sought to get the floor, and there was such an uproar that the meeting broke up in confusion.

Even under the best of circumstances, the lily-black candidates had never had a chance of polling a substantial vote, but the inability of the Negroes to unite behind them doomed whatever possibility there had been for a creditable showing. Mitchell and his fellow nominees got 5,046 votes. E. Lee Trinkle, the winning Democratic candidate, polled 139,416, and Henry W. Anderson, the Republican, 65,933. Mitchell presumably had not expected a greatly different result, and he doubtless felt that the blacks had gotten across the point that they were disgusted with their treatment by the Republicans.

The president of the Mechanics Bank appeared to be riding high, when suddenly in 1922 the bank collapsed and was ordered to close by the state. It never reopened. There were various theories as to the causes for the bank's failure. Some blacks argued that "John Mitchell's enemies got even with him by breaking his bank," while others contended that "the white people who resented him swore that they had to get this man, and well, they got him."

Abram L. Harris, a Richmond-born black, analyzed the problem dispassionately in his book, *The Negro as Capitalist*. He concluded that the State Corporation Commission must have known for years that the Mechanics Bank was unstable but did nothing, "either because they respected Mitchell and therefore gave him as much latitude as they could under the law, or because they felt it did not matter what a Negro banker did." Harris said the bank "suffered from benign neglect." He declared, further, that it had an unsound "investment and credit policy" that kept it "always in a frozen condition," since "in no year during its existence were the bank's fixed assets under 150 per cent of capital investments," whereas "the normal rate is 21 per cent for state banks." One of the bank's most costly white elephants was a theater on Broad Street, "held as a matter of race pride."

Harris made the following statement concerning certain gross irregularities in the bank's affairs: "At least $100,000 in deposits did not appear on the bank's ledger, and it was discovered that dummies were frequently used to cover up misappropriations of the bank's funds. The receivers reported that 'discrepancies of every conceivable nature were noted' in the deposit records." Numerous examples were given. The report of the state bank examiner declared that the causes of the bank's closing included "an unsound investment policy, mismanagement, falsification of records and dishonesty."

President Mitchell was indicted and tried in Hustings Court. He was convicted of false and fraudulent entries, with intent to defraud the bank. He appealed, however, and the Virginia Supreme Court held that there was failure to prove the existence of "false and fraudulent entries." The high court also stated that there were other errors at the trial. The criminal prosecution was accordingly quashed, and that was the end of the matter as far as Mitchell's trial was concerned. Abram Harris concludes, "It seems that Mitchell made good the claims against him, and as a result died a virtually poor man" in 1929.

It was a sad dénouement for a citizen who, in other respects, had achieved a very creditable public record. His career as a newspaperman had been exceptional, and he had exhibited great courage in taking unpopular stands on public issues. His editorials were highly articulate and trenchant. John Mitchell, Jr., was probably the most admired black journalist of his time, and he achieved this against great odds, financial and otherwise. In 1977 he was honored when the Society of Professional Journalists, Sigma Delta Chi, unveiled a marker on the *Afro-American* and *Planet* Building at 301 East Clay Street, dedicating it as an historic site in journalism. This was the site of the *Planet* when it was directed by Mitchell, and the marker recognized his distinguished contribution. The following year Mitchell was one of five black newspaper publishers enshrined in Howard University's Black Press Archives and Gallery. And in 1986 his name was on the first list of journalists elected to the newly established Virginia Commonwealth University Mass Communications Hall of Fame.

CHAPTER EIGHT

JOSEPH BRYAN OF THE *TIMES*

J oseph Bryan of Richmond was probably the most admired Virginian of his day. He was extremely active in many different capacities—as businessman, civic leader, churchman, and philanthropist—but the period of his public life that meant most to him was when he served as the crusading editor and publisher of the Richmond *Times*.

Major Lewis Ginter owned the *Times* briefly, but he lost interest as well as money in the enterprise. So he gave it to his friend Joe Bryan in 1887. "Then began by all odds the most entrancing period of Joseph Bryan's public activities," his son John Stewart Bryan wrote in his memoir of his father, *Joseph Bryan, His Times, His Family, His Friends.* "He had not the least idea how to make a paper profitable, but he immediately made the *Times* powerful. To courage, brilliance, and absolute freedom of action he added a passionate devotion to an ideal Virginia that offered no possible place for chicanery or corruption." The tribute is that of an adoring son, but it is justified. On certain aspects of the race question Joseph Bryan was ultraconservative, but his motives and his integrity were seldom if ever questioned.

Widespread fraud in elections, for which the whites who controlled the Democratic party were primarily responsible; the nomination of William Jennings Bryan for the presidency on a "free silver" platform in 1896; and a challenge to a duel—these were the crucial events in the journalistic career of Joseph Bryan. He met each of these issues head-on. Although a member of the state Democratic committee, he assailed the party's leadership for its role in promoting electoral fraud, and was loudly denounced as a renegade. The free silver movement impressed him as "anarchy and socialism," and he led in putting the rival Palmer-Buckner "Gold Democrat" presidential ticket into the field, thereby bringing down on his head an avalanche of abuse, accompanied by a large drop in the circulation of the *Times*. And when the paper published something which brought him a challenge to "the field of honor," he courageously announced that he had no intention of fighting a duel, since he considered dueling "absurd and barbarous." The result was the end of dueling in Virginia.

The eighth child of John Randolph Bryan and Elizabeth Tucker Coalter Bryan, Joseph Bryan was born in their home, Eagle Point, Gloucester County, Virginia, on August 13, 1845. His mother was the favorite niece of John Randolph of Roanoke, who was also the guardian of John Randolph Bryan, Randolph's namesake.

Eagle Point lay on the Severn River, and young Bryan was one of a group of what a member of the family termed "water rats." The principal diversions of Joe and his brother St. George were "fishing, crabbing, swimming, sailing, or as landsmen, riding, shooting marsh hens, following their father as he hunted quail in company with his friends." Joe Bryan was educated at first by tutors (as well as a dancing master) at Eagle Point. At age eleven, in 1856, he was sent off to the Episcopal High School near Alexandria, which at that time was in a most primitive state of development. The rising bell sounded at five in summer and six in winter, facilities for bathing were almost nonexistent, the dismal dormitories were dimly lighted by a few oil lamps, and the boys were whipped for infractions of the rules. Joe Bryan and Jeff Phelps were the two youngest lads in school, and to homesickness was added the ordeal which the entire state underwent when blizzards in the winter of 1856–57 made it the bitterest in Virginia history. Bryan never forgot the kindness and loving sympathy of Mrs. John P. McGuire, wife of the headmaster, in those difficult days.

He was a student at the school for five years and made a highly creditable record. Upon the instructions of Headmaster McGuire the entire student body left on May 3, 1861, when Union troops were about to occupy Alexandria. Joe was barely sixteen, and his parents forbade him to enlist in the Confederate forces until he was eighteen, the lawful age of enlistment. He accordingly entered the University of Virginia in October 1862, at which time there were only forty-six students—those who were wounded or otherwise unfit for military service, and the very young.

When the university closed for the summer in 1863, Joe Bryan's eighteenth birthday was only a couple of months away. He was eager to get into the fighting but had the misfortune to break his left wrist badly in a fall. A serious fracture, it was clumsily set by an incompetent physician. The healing process was slow and painful. As a result he had to be content with a temporary assignment with the Nitre and Mining Bureau at Dublin, Virginia, an agency vital to the supply of powder for the Confederate forces. At the bureau he was given the temporary rank of captain.

In May, 1864, Joe managed to get a furlough and he set out at once for Lee's army on the Rapidan. He served until June 1 as a private in the Richmond Howitzers, and took part in the bloody fighting around Spotsylvania Courthouse. But his furlough ended and he returned to the bureau in southwest Virginia. By the fall his arm was sufficiently healed for him to handle the bridle of a horse, and he succeeded in joining Colonel John S. Mosby's renowned partisans.

Mosby's fame by that time was nationwide. With an incredibly small force of horsemen, and by the use of astounding bravado and cold nerve, he had succeeded in keeping far larger Union forces bewildered and off balance throughout the area known as "Mosby's Confederacy" in northern Virginia. Among the amazing feats of this band of a few hundred intrepid fighting men was the seizure of a Union train near Harper's Ferry carrying approximately $173,000, and the capture by a band of thirty, led by Mosby, of Union General E. H. Stoughton, with one hundred men and many horses, at Fairfax Courthouse. Of the latter episode, Mosby wrote: "A light was struck, and on the bed we saw the general sleeping as soundly as the Turk when Marco Bozzaris waked him up. There was no time for ceremony, so I drew up the bedclothes, pulled up the general's shirt, and gave him a spank on his bare back, and told him to get up." What happened next is described by John Esten Cooke, who said Stoughton sat up and demanded, "Do you know who I am sir?" "Do you know Mosby, general?" said Mosby. "Yes, " was the eager response, "Have you got the —— rascal?" "No, " replied Mosby, "but he has got you!" Such feats as the foregoing had made John S. Mosby a hero and a paladin throughout the South.

Young Bryan's excitement at joining so renowned a Confederate unit can be imagined. At Ashby's Gap, soon after his arrival, he asked his friend Charlie Dear, one of Mosby's men, how he could make a reputation in the command. Dear replied that they were about to charge the Yankees in a few minutes, and all Joe had to do was to break away from the ranks and ride full speed ahead toward the enemy. This he proceeded to do, according to Colonel Mosby, who said Bryan, "whipping out his revolver and digging spurs into his horse, went flying down the mountain full tilt into the face of that powerful enemy, letting out a rebel yell that must have been heard across the Alleghenies.... Single-handed he was charging a full regiment of Sheridan's veteran cavalry." But "before Joe Bryan got within a hundred yards of the enemy's column, they had halted, faltered and turned tail, spurring full speed for the valley camps."

This was written by Mosby in 1911, a half-century later, and the details may have been somewhat exaggerated. John M. Munson, a member of the command, described the episode in less colorful terms in his *Reminiscences*. Both accounts agree, however, that Bryan charged recklessly and fearlessly as soon as the order was given. Captain Mountjoy seems to have been close behind him, and both of them might have been killed or captured if the regiment of Federal cavalry had not wheeled and galloped back in support of the infantry and artillery.

Mountjoy was greatly impressed with Bryan, saying "he won his spurs in the first round." The youth was accordingly given the distinction of riding for the rest of the war "in the first four of Company D." About a week later he was wounded twice in a fight near Upperville. After a period of convalescence he went back to the command in December, 1864, and served until the surrender.

Like thousands of other almost penniless Confederate soldiers, Bryan struggled back to his home, and shortly thereafter matriculated again at the University of Virginia. In that institution he had an excellent record, in both the academic and law schools. In 1868 he hung out his shingle as an attorney in Palmyra, county seat of Fluvanna. He chose tiny, bucolic Palmyra instead of Richmond because he had no money to pay for food and lodging, and by launching his practice there he could live at the nearby family home, Carysbrook.

Bryan managed to scratch out a sufficient living from his Palmyra office to marry Miss Belle Stewart of Brook Hill, a member of a prominent Henrico County family. She would be a tower of strength for him throughout his career. Mrs. Bryan became a leader in many civic endeavors, and was noted for her charming and gracious personality.

In 1872 Bryan opened a law office in Richmond at 1002 East Main Street, and his career took off. In the year following he was a candidate for the House of Delegates on the Conservative party ticket. The Conservative party was chiefly interested at that time in white supremacy, and the Negro vote went solidly for the opposition. Bryan was defeated. In 1875 he was asked to run again by a substantial group of citizens, who published a large advertisement in the *Dispatch* urging this thirty-year-old lawyer to become a candidate. He acceded to their request but lost again. The winning candidate, R. H. Talley, got 1,409 votes, T. W. Hoeninger got 1,290, and Bryan got 1,289. In his political innocence, Bryan had voted for his opponent, Hoeninger, while his opponent had voted for himself— which accounted for the margin of one.

Two years passed, and Bryan's admirers again placed an advertisement in the *Dispatch* urging him to run, requesting that he give his views on the state debt question, the hot issue of the time. He again agreed to become a candidate, and was his always forthright self in expressing his strong opposition to William Mahone's effort to "readjust" Virginia's debt. "Any conduct on the part of Virginia inconsistent with her solemn promises is fraught not only with disgrace and shame, but with serious injury to the material welfare of the whole state," he declared. Once again he was defeated by a small margin. It was his last try for public office.

These losses at the polls seem to have had no adverse effect on Joseph Bryan's rapid rise to a position of unrivaled leadership in the community, or on his acquisition of substantial wealth. His father-in-law had insisted that, until he was able to construct an adequate home of his own, he and his bride live at Brook Hill, and they did so, except when they were at Carysbrook near Palmyra. In 1885, however, Bryan built Laburnum, on the site of the Lyons home that had burned during the Civil War. Two years later Major Ginter gave him the ailing *Times*, and the most exciting and rewarding period of his public career began.

Page McCarty, who had mortally wounded John Mordecai in their famous duel fourteen years before over the beautiful Mary Triplett, was editor of the *Times* when Bryan took over the paper. Herbert T. Ezekiel, a reporter there, has left an intriguing vignette of this duelist. "Of course, everyone in the office stood in righteous fear of Captain McCarty. To my utter surprise, he seemed as gentle as a woman.... There is little doubt that McCarty never had a moment's happiness after the duel, and that he deliberately sought death.... Beneath his stern exterior McCarty carried the kindest of hearts." He had been active in newspaper publishing in Lynchburg and Richmond in the middle eighties but without success.

McCarty was not retained as editor of the *Times*. Bryan took the editor's title himself and named William L. ("Buck") Royall chief editorial writer. Royall wrote most of the editorials, but Bryan "always directed," and kept in close touch with the editorial side. His personality and views were stamped all over the paper, and when moved to do so he could write with the best of them, forcefully and gracefully. He also realized the importance of obtaining the best mechanical equipment. He was the first publisher south of the Potomac to install a Mergenthaler Linotype, a great innovation in a time when setting type by hand was still the rule.

The widespread skulduggery indulged in by both major parties in Virginia elections was a scandal that provoked expressions of outrage in Joseph Bryan's *Times*. Elections were being stolen right and left, ballot boxes were being stuffed, bribery was frequent, and other shenanigans were winked at. Although a member of the state Democratic committee, Bryan lashed out through his newspaper at the manner in which Democrats were participating in these practices. The rival *Dispatch* accused him of being a traitor to the Democratic party. The Anderson-McCormick law had been passed to legalize fraud in elections, the *Times* asserted. The courthouse cliques, manned almost exclusively by Democrats, were deeply involved in the corruption. It was the railroad era, and the roads were up to their necks in politics. They were greasing the palms of candidates for office from both parties, the paper said.

Many Democratic papers joined the *Dispatch* in expressing horror that another supposed party organ, the *Times*, should voice such heretical sentiments, but this did not deter Bryan. He went right ahead denouncing the crooked elections and those responsible for them. When J. Thomas Goode ran for Congress from Southside, Virginia, the *Times* said he was defeated because the overwhelmingly Democratic county returning boards threw out the entire vote in thirty-one of ninety-eight precincts for such ridiculous reasons as the sealing up of ballots and poll books in one package instead of two. The paper charged that the election officials had acted in obeisance to "some secret and central influence and inspiration," and that "the Goode case has brought into public view the most monstrous and dangerous perversion of tyrannical authority." The domination of Virginia politics by the "courthouse cliques" meant "a tyranny and corrupt domination of us no whit inferior to that which Mahone imposed on the state," the *Times* snorted.

The defeat of Fitzhugh Lee for the U.S. Senate by Thomas S. Martin in 1893 was seen by the *Times* as another example of the kind of insidious politics that had no place in Virginia. Fitzhugh Lee, a nephew of "Marse Robert," had fought with great credit as a general in the Civil War, had served well as governor of Virginia, and was widely known and extremely popular. Martin was a country lawyer from Scottsville who represented the Chesapeake and Ohio Railway in Albemarle and adjacent counties. At the outset it appeared that it would be no contest, with Lee a sure winner, but this conventional wisdom was based on totally erroneous assumptions. U.S. senators were elected by the state legislature at that time, and for many months Martin and his agents had been working quietly with members of the General Assembly. When the votes were counted, Martin led on the first ballot, and won with considerable ease on the sixth.

How did it happen? Allen W. Moger writes in *Virginia: Bourbonism to Byrd*:

> That Tom Martin was elected . . . by shrewd organization and the use of railroad money by railroad men is overwhelmingly supported by contemporary evidence, private correspondence and subsequent developments. . . . Martin would not have been elected . . . without the power of railroad money and influence. . . . That none [of Martin's backers] saw anything wrong with the political practices of the railroads in the campaigns of 1891 and 1893 reflected the dominant political thinking of the times.

But Joseph Bryan saw a great deal that was wrong. His paper led in charging irregularities in the Martin-Lee contest. Moger says that Bryan "did not object to the railroads' practice of giving money to the Democratic party, but he was distressed by evidence that the railroads were distributing money through their own agents for one candidate and outside the regular channels of the party." The *Times* declared that it "would rather see every railroad in the state torn up before it will permit them to interfere with elections by corrupting the suffrage with money."

The uproar over the role of the railroads in the Martin-Lee

election had hardly died down when the presidential campaign of 1896 brought William Jennings Bryan and free silver to the fore. Joseph Bryan (no relation) and the *Times* were in the van once more in denouncing the Democratic nominee and all that he stood for. The convention that nominated W. J. Bryan after his "cross of gold" speech was termed by the *Times* "the most emotional, hysterical, irrational body of its size," and the paper added that the convention "nominated a mere youth ... because he rattled off before it a studied piece of sophomorical rodomontade that did not contain a single sound proposition, and abounded in nonsense and anarchy in equal proportions." The newspaper denounced "all forms of Populistic paternalism and anarchistic incendiarism."

Nevertheless, the measure that W. J. Bryan and the Democratic party were peddling, "free and unlimited coinage of silver at 16 to 1," was enormously popular in Virginia and elsewhere. The terrible depression of the nineties was at its height, and everyone was casting about for ways to end the misery and put people back to work. As an example of how acute the crisis was, consider the plight of Virginia's Northern Neck area. There was not a single bank in that historic region, and the inhabitants were reduced to barter or the use of eggs or coon skins for currency. Thousands believed that free silver was the answer, and anyone who spoke out publicly against it was sure to be cordially hated.

Such considerations did not deter Joseph Bryan. He took the lead in organizing a "sound money" convention of "Gold Democrats" or "Gold Bugs" at Richmond, and he presided over the gathering. Some three hundred delegates from the cities and towns of the state attended. A platform endorsing the gold standard was adopted, and the Palmer-Buckner ticket of the so-called National Democrats was endorsed.

Virginia's free silverites were infuriated. Old friends of Joseph

Bryan cut him on the street, men shook their fists at one another in public, and speakers against the supposed panacea were hissed from platforms. The *Times* had built up a circulation of 7,000, but its readership suffered a precipitous drop as cancellations rolled in. Irate citizens picked the paper up with fire tongs rather than touch it with their hands. A preposterous rumor was circulated that the paper had been "bought with British gold."

Candidate William Jennings Bryan spoke in Richmond to what was said to be the largest political gathering in Virginia history. On election night the report was circulated by the free silverites that the *Times* was planning to defeat their candidate by "holding back the returns"—just how this feat was to be managed was not explained. Feeling ran so high that a mob formed outside the newspaper building and threatened violence. Joseph Bryan sat imperturbably at his desk, and the police maintained control of the situation.

When the votes were counted, it was found that Palmer and Buckner had gotten exactly 2,127 votes in Virginia—a far from impressive showing. The gold Democrats didn't run well anywhere. William McKinley, the winning Republican candidate, apparently got most of the votes of those Democrats who saw the fallacies in free silver. Joseph Bryan was disappointed, but he never regretted fighting this or any other fight when he regarded the issue as being of transcendent importance. He took his financial losses on the *Times* philosophically. And many of the friends that he seemed to lose during the campaign were not permanently alienated. U.S. Senator John W. Daniel, the "lame lion of Lynchburg," and leader of the free silverites, is an example. He and Joe Bryan soon forgot their differences and maintained an amicable correspondence in the succeeding years.

Only a few Virginia papers joined the *Times* in its crusade. One of the most militant supporters of William Jennings Bryan was Carter Glass, editor and publisher of the Lynchburg *News*.

Glass was young, redheaded, and fiery when he went to the Democratic National Convention at Chicago in 1896. Carried away by Bryan's "cross of gold" speech, he grabbed the Virginia standard and rushed to join the parade for the "Boy Orator of the Platte." In the campaign that followed, his *News* was almost hysterical in its advocacy of free silver and in its excoriation of all who opposed the program. Its violent attacks on the "gold cormorants" and the "banded money sharks of Wall Street" and its apostrophes to "the toiling millions" sounded almost like the latter-day tirades of the Communist *Daily Worker*. Many years afterward, as a U.S. senator, Glass continued to be vituperative in controversy, and he was very much so in denouncing President Franklin D. Roosevelt for abandoning the gold standard. In direct contrast to his own enthusiastic espousal of free silver some forty years before, he pronounced Roosevelt's abandonment of the gold standard "worse than anything Ali Baba and his forty thieves ever perpetrated."

The race issue was, of course, much to the fore in the late nineteenth century, and the attitude of the *Times* was by no means liberal by modern standards. Only a generation had passed since the end of the war and the elimination of slavery, and the great majority of blacks were illiterate, thanks in large part to the fact that it had been illegal to educate them as slaves.

Although the *Times* was not as insulting as the *Dispatch* in its references to the freemen, one of its reporters "gleefully described the various 'shades' and 'tints' of all the 'coons' at a meeting at which John Mitchell presided." Mitchell's *Planet* frequently "attacked the *Times* for its 'severe spasms' of 'Negrophobia', which, if briefer than those of the *Dispatch*, were nearly as violent," Ann F. Alexander wrote. Peter J. Burton, a *Dispatch* reporter, described the blacks regularly in derogatory language. According to Alexander, however, the *Times* was "without doubt the paper preferred by the city's blacks."

When the state constitutional convention of 1901–02 convened, the *Times* had been carrying on a seven-year crusade for honest elections. Bryan said, concerning the methods that had been used to disfranchise the blacks: "I had rather see the Democrats take shotguns and drive the Negroes from the polls than to see our young men cheat. If they once have learned that lesson...they will not stop at cheating Negroes." A major objective of the constitutional convention was to disfranchise most of the blacks by legal means instead of "cheating" them. It was argued that honest elections would thereby be promoted. Joseph Bryan, who was against political skulduggery in all its forms, objected strongly to the dishonest methods by which blacks were being kept from voting. The great majority of the Negroes were effectively prevented from voting by the $1.50 poll tax, payable three years in a row and six months before any election, and by other restrictions placed in the new constitution. Not only was Bryan in favor of this poll tax, but the *Times* demanded in 1900 that a rigid principle of segregation be "applied in every relation of Southern life," on the ground that "God Almighty drew the color line, and it cannot be obliterated."

However, "there was a deep and instinctive understanding" between Bryan and the blacks, according to his son. The latter wrote in his memoirs of an episode that occurred on a Pullman car en route to St. Paul, Minnesota, about 1885. The porter came to Joseph Bryan and said, "Your berth is ready, sir." Bryan demanded of the porter why he had made up his berth when "there are many ladies and children on the train, and you ought to have looked after them first."

"I know sir," said the porter, "but I jes made up yo' berth fust bekaze you speaks that lovely language."

"Where do you come from, boy?"

"Columbia, Fluvanna County," said the porter.

"Good heavens," was the reply, "no wonder you like to hear me talk; that's my home too."

It will be noted that the porter was addressed as "boy," unfortunately a widespread habit of white men in dealing with grown blacks in that era and for many years thereafter.

A strange sequel to the stand of the *Times* for segregation "in every relation of Southern life" was the fact that some years later, when William L. Royall, who wrote most of the paper's editorials, had retired from journalism, he evidently underwent a complete change of heart. Files of the National Association for the Advancement of Colored People show that he cooperated quietly with that organization in its efforts to break down segregation in housing and sought to make it possible for blacks to live wherever they wished in Richmond.

Royall was succeeded on the *Times* by W. S. Copeland, an amazingly prolific editorial writer. Copeland not only produced the editorials for the *Times*; he also wrote those for the *Leader*, which Bryan had acquired—thus filling the editorial columns in thirteen different issues of the two papers each week.

Bryan remained a staunch friend of Confederate Colonel John S. Mosby after the Civil War—this despite Mosby's apostasy in turning Republican, which made him extremely unpopular throughout the South. Nor did his characteristically biting comment on Bryan's support in the *Times* of the role of the United States in the Spanish-American War mar their friendship. Mosby, who became increasingly critical of the South in the postwar era, was similarly caustic in his references to the behavior of the United States in the Philippines. His pungent comment on Bryan's attitude was expressed as follows: "Joe ... says it is a duty we owe not only to ourselves but to the Phillipinos [*sic*] to murder them because they refuse to acknowledge the validity of their sale to us at two dollars a head.... These people are hypocrites." Despite these biting words, Bryan besought President Theodore Roosevelt to give his old commander a federal job.

One of the greatest services performed by Joseph Bryan was his courageous action in giving the *coup de grace* to dueling, not only in Virginia but apparently throughout the South. In 1893 Bryan was challenged by Jefferson D. Wallace of Richmond, who resented something that had appeared in the *Times*. Bryan replied that he would not accept a challenge for three reasons: he professed to be a Christian, and the idea of settling a controversy by a duel "is utterly abhorrent"; he was a law-abiding citizen, and dueling was illegal; and, finally, dueling was "absurd and barbarous." Whereas Wallace had said that it was "the redress which obtains among gentlemen," Bryan retorted that it "no longer 'obtains among gentlemen', and never should have done so." He turned Wallace over to the police, who arrested him. The charge was not pressed, but that was the end of the "code of honor" in Virginia. Bryan was overwhelmed with congratulations.

Dueling, it must be admitted, was on the way out by the 1890s. The nonsensical idea that disputes, however trivial, should be settled by unlimbering one's arsenal was coming to be regarded as the imbecility that it was. As William Oliver Stevens wrote in *Pistols at Ten Paces*: "Men shot each other for gambling debts, for a dispute over billiards, an uncomplimentary word in an editorial, a jest at table, a refusal to take a glass of whiskey, or, most of all, for disagreements in politics. Almost never, however, did they fight over a woman."

Barnwell Rhett of South Carolina, a noted political fire-eater, had taken his political life in his hands in 1852 by declaring to the U.S. Senate, when baited and insulted by Jeremiah Clemens, an Alabama "cooperationist," that he "feared God more than man and would not fight a duel." This was a horrifying doctrine in that era, and dueling continued unabated. We have noted the action of James C. Southall, editor of the Richmond *Enquirer*, in announcing in 1872 that he would never fight a duel, despite what he termed "cowardly recriminations" against him from

Alexander Moseley, editor of the *Whig*. Challenges continued, nevertheless. John S. Wise fought in 1882, but neither participant was injured; and Wise declared publicly that he would never, under any conditions, fight again on "the field of honor." Like Bryan, Wise had a fine record as a Confederate soldier. When in 1884 Page McCarty attacked him as "a jackass, with apologies to the jackass," Wise took occasion to remind his readers that he had announced two years before that he would never fight another duel.

Wise also made a scathing attack on McCarty: "Unmarried, penniless, without any fixed employment, dissipated, with nothing to lose, he seems possessed of a devil, and would no doubt esteem it a mercy for some gentleman to kill him and ease his tortured brain and conscience.... I have tried not to be too severe upon poor McCarty, whose wasted talents and miserable life I truly pity." The fearless action of John S. Wise, who had fought with the VMI cadets at New Market, went far to convince the public that dueling was on the toboggan. But it was not until Joseph Bryan refused a challenge that this senseless custom was ended, once and for all.

The *Times* was widely recognized for its high quality. The New York *Sun* complimented it as "in every way a good newspaper," but said that "when it describes itself as 'intensely Southern' we do not understand what it means." Bryan wrote a long editorial in reply, the concluding paragraph of which sums up the position well:

The curse of slavery has been removed. The agitation which it produced has ended, and the Union is assured. For all this they, and we, who have survived the war have every reason to be thankful, but for the millions who went down in brokenhearted poverty to their graves for causes they neither produced nor could control, our sympathy will ever overflow, and whenever their fate is in any way recalled, we are and always will be "intensely Southern."

Bryan was at all times quick to defend the South and what it fought for. When the New York *Mail & Express* published several insulting editorials concerning the region, the *Times* termed the New York editor "a miserable hypocrite."

Reference has been made to Bryan's acquisition in 1896 of the *Leader*, a paper published in Manchester. Then in 1903 he bought the *Dispatch* from John L. Williams & Sons, and combined it with the *Times* to form the *Times-Dispatch*. Simultaneously he sold the *Leader* to John L. Williams & Sons, who already owned the Richmond *News*, and these two papers were combined to form the *News Leader*. Thus, for the time being, the *Times-Dispatch* monopolized the morning field in Richmond and the *News Leader* the evening. In 1908, Bryan acquired the *News Leader* and hence was publisher of both papers. He died in that year, and soon thereafter there were other changes in the ownership of Richmond's daily press.

Bryan outlined his newspaper creed in an address to the Virginia Press Association. He said, in part:

> The newspaper editor should feel himself a consecrated man. Consecrated above all to truth. Consecrated to justice, feeling that not only is he restrained from the defense of an unworthy cause by his own obligations to duty, but that, as the greatest reverence is due to those who look to him for guidance, he should feel as the pilot who steers the ship through treacherous channels, with precious and confiding souls in his care.

For some reason, he had a low opinion of most newspapermen, despite his devotion to their craft. Even more surprising, in view of his role as one of the leading laymen in the Episcopal Church, was his unfavorable opinion of preachers. John Stewart Bryan, his son, quoted him as having said "over and over":

> I have been a soldier, a mule trader, a lawyer, a railroad president and builder, and still am a director; I have mined coal and iron, operated pig iron smelters, built locomotives, developed real estate, run street car lines; I have had intimate association with bankers, brokers, doctors, lawyers and newspapermen, and have taken an active part in the work of the Episcopal Church. So I think I have sufficient background to form an opinion, and I unhesitatingly put lawyers at the top and newspapermen at the bottom of all the men that I have ever known, and preachers next to newspapermen!

On one occasion he remarked that "the Christian religion must be divine, because it has survived the preachers." Yet he was a leader in his church's general conventions, and a delegate to the Lambeth Conference in England. On attending a Confederate reunion, he said, "A Confederate reunion moves me more than anything on earth except religion."

The almost unbelievable variety of Joseph Bryan's business and civic interests makes it all the more remarkable that he was able to devote so much time and thought to journalism. His energy was astounding. A diary kept by his wife shows that he was involved in countless meetings, conventions, and sessions of various kinds, and traveled many times each month to New York and other cities. When at home he was a hospitable host, entertaining many guests at Laburnum.

In 1896, in the middle of the great depression of the nineties, the pressmen at the *Times* threatened to strike for higher wages. His reaction was as follows:

I have had this paper since 1887 and have paid you your wages every week; you neither knew nor cared what it cost me to meet those charges, yet now, because you think you can extort money from me, you threaten a strike. Before I will yield to any such coercion I will take an axe and break that press to pieces and throw it into the James River. And let me tell you one thing. After the battle of Spotsylvania I had had no food for two days, and I found a dead Yankee who had some rotten pork in his hand. I took a ramrod and fished it out and ate it, and I can do it again. And if you can't do it, don't go to war with me.

There was no strike. If the foregoing sounds strident, it should be noted on Bryan's behalf that the stresses and strains of the terrible depression were approximately as severe on him as they were on everybody else, and it was hardly the proper time for the pressmen to threaten him.

Bryan's concern for his employees was evident in many ways, as in a strike at about the same time at the American Locomotive Works in Richmond, of which he was managing director. He sent money privately to help the families of strikers who were in need. When one of his business friends said that he thought this most unwise, since it "prolongs the strike," Bryan replied, "My God! Don't you know you cannot let women and children starve?"

When a subsequent depression struck in the early 1900s, the New York office of the American Locomotive Works decreed that there should be a cut in salaries. Bryan wrote in reply: "You are paying me $10,000 a year as managing director; I don't need it and I am not sure that I earn it. What I wish you to do is to take my adjusted salary and divide it among the boys here; they need it and I want them to have it."

Such acts as these endeared Joe Bryan to those who knew him. A severe attack of typhoid fever, one of the great killers of that era, laid him low temporarily in 1900 and weakened his heart. When he recovered as fully as possible, he resumed his furious pace, directing the *Times* and handling several other jobs, traveling frequently and giving his time and energy to a great variety of causes. Finally, his weakened heart gave way, and he died November 20, 1908.

There was a great outpouring of heartfelt tributes from persons in all walks of life. He was buried in the churchyard of Emmanuel Church, Brook Hill, where he and his family had long been active, and where some months later a window to his memory from "his friends and fellow-laborers on the *Times-Dispatch*" was dedicated. Journalism had been his first and greatest love, and the feeling was reciprocated. In the following year, the congregation of Abingdon Church, Gloucester County, where he had been baptized as a baby, and where he had served as a vestryman in his last years, placed a tablet in his honor. The climactic tribute came in 1911 when a life-size statue was erected in Monroe Park, Richmond, an almost unprecedented accolade for a private citizen. The pedestal of the monument bore the following inscription:

TO EXALTED CITIZENSHIP
IN THE PRIVATE WALKS
OF LIFE
AS ILLUSTRATED
BY THE CAREER OF
JOSEPH BRYAN
THIS STATUE IS DEDICATED
BY THE PEOPLE OF RICHMOND
THE CHARACTER OF THE CITIZEN
IS THE STRENGTH OF THE STATE

Joseph Bryan risked the very existence of the Richmond *Times* and his own fiscal solvency in attacking free silver with ferocity in 1896, when this supposed panacea for the business panic then raging was enormously popular. He was similarly fearless in denouncing, over a period of years, the crooked elections in Virginia, controlled and manipulated by some of his best friends in the Democratic party. A man of unshakable integrity and exceptional charm, he was widely respected, even by those who disagreed with him. The youth who as one of Mosby's rangers sought to charge a regiment of Sheridan's veterans almost single-handedly, grew up to become a man who "never turned his back but marched breast forward." He left his mark on his generation.

L'ENVOI

There are, of course, numerous other Virginia editors, both in the capital city of Richmond and elsewhere in the state, who made important contributions to the history and the life of the Old Dominion. Were this account to be carried on into the twentieth century, a whole new cast of characters would move onto the stage, some of them as influential, although not as colorful, as those I have discussed. But that is another story, and it moreover has to do with a journalistic profession that is far changed from flatbed presses, hand-set type, and four-page newspapers whose news and editorial commentary were so mixed that the distinction between facts and opinion was at times all but indistinguishable.

Today's newspapers are in every way superior to those of the old days. However partisan and impassioned the political and social views of today's publisher and editor may be, a strict separation between news and opinion is usually rigorously enforced. In many instances, the editor of a newspaper has little or nothing to do with anything but editorial opinion; all the rest of the vast apparatus of news, features, advertising, circulation, and production involved in the delivery of a modern newspaper to its subscribers is the responsibility of others. The publication of even a small daily newspaper today is a business enterprise costing in the millions of dollars. The days when an ambitious young man could raise a few thousand dollars, hire a couple of printers, purchase a hand-fed, hand-inked, hand-operated Washington handpress and set out to lecture community, state, and nation on their sins has long since departed, and mostly for the best.

Yet the profession of newspaperman remains, I think, not only honorable but vital to our society; and it is important to remember that the achievements of today's journalists and journalism are built solidly and squarely upon the labors of just such persons as those whose careers have been chronicled in this book. The old Virginia editor—opinionative, excitable, partisan, prone to exaggeration, and liable for the defense of his opinions at ten paces—gave voice and vigor to the thoughts and emotions of his constituency, and said what he thought. We may wince sometimes at the abusiveness of his discourse, deplore his recklessness of expression, admire his courage and marvel at his zeal, but we ought never to forget what he was, or how he plied his profession.

Virginia newspapers were a primary source for this book. Among them were the Richmond *Enquirer, Whig, Examiner, Dispatch, Times,* and *Planet*; the Norfolk *Ledger, Landmark, Dispatch, Pilot,* and *Virginian*; the Lynchburg *Virginian*; and the Petersburg *Index.* The *Virginia Gazette* of Williamsburg was also a source, as was the *Southern Literary Messenger.*

Allen W. Moger's *Virginia: Bourbonism to Byrd, 1875–1925* (Charlottesville: Univ. Press of Virginia, 1968) is an able study of political, economic, and journalistic developments in the post-bellum era. Railroad development with its attendant stresses and strains, the heated controversy surrounding the state debt, and the uproar over "free silver" are examined.

Another book dealing with the period that was frequently consulted was Lenoir Chambers and Joseph E. Shanks' *Salt Water and Printer's Ink* (Chapel Hill: Univ. of North Carolina Press, 1967). It was extremely useful for the Norfolk scene and for the careers of William E. Cameron, John Hampden Pleasants, and William C. Elam, each of whom was a newspaper editor in Norfolk, as well as in one or more other Virginia cities.

Charles C. Pearson's *The Readjuster Movement in Virginia* (Gloucester, Mass.: Peter Smith, 1969) provides an incisive analysis of the controversy surrounding payment of the state debt.

Two books that are valuable for the light that they shed on racial attitudes of the press and the public are Charles E. Wynes' *Race Relations in Virginia, 1870–1902* (Charlottesville: Univ. Press of Virginia, 1961), and Alrutheus A. Taylor's *The Negro in the Reconstruction of Virginia* (Washington, D.C.: Association for the Study of Negro Life and History, 1926).

Two important works on the code duello are William Oliver Stevens' *Pistols at Ten Paces* (Boston: Houghton Mifflin, 1940) and A. W. Patterson's *The Code Duello* (Richmond: Richmond Press Inc., 1927). The latter work is especially informative as to several Virginia duels.

Lester J. Cappon's remarkably complete *Richmond Newspapers: 1821–1935* (New York: Appleton-Century, 1936) lists editors, publishers, and other essential details for every Richmond paper over a period of more than a century.

Principal sources for the editorial careers examined in detail in this volume are as follows:

The leading source on Thomas Ritchie is Charles H. Ambler's *Thomas Ritchie: A Study in Virginia Politics* (Richmond: Bell Book & Stationery Co., 1913). This work is also useful for the light that it sheds on Ritchie's rivalry with John Hampden Pleasants, and various events of the first half of the nineteenth century. Details concerning the duel of Thomas Ritchie, Jr., with Pleasants are given in *A Full Report Embracing All the Evidence and Arguments in the Case of the Commonwealth of Virginia vs. Thomas Ritchie, Jr.* (New York: Burgess, Stringer & Co., 1846).

Information on Pleasants' career was somewhat difficult to

find, despite its brilliance. The address of Robert W. Hughes, "Editors of the Past," delivered to the Virginia Press Association on June 22, 1897 (Richmond: William Ellis Jones, 1897), was extremely helpful. The same is true of an article by John A. Parker entitled "The Missing Link," which appeared originally in the Norfolk *Landmark* and was reprinted in the *National Quarterly Review*, July, 1880 (Washington, D.C.: Gray & Clarkson, 1886).

John M. Daniel's bellicose career on the Richmond *Examiner* is described by Robert W. Hughes, his associate on that paper, in Hughes' address to the Virginia Press Association referred to above. George W. Bagby's delightful essay "John M. Daniel's Latch-Key," from Bagby's *The Old Virginia Gentleman and Other Sketches*, ed. Ellen M. Bagby, 4th edition (Richmond: Dietz Press, 1943), is also by a newspaper associate of Daniel. And Daniel's brother, Frederick S. Daniel, provides further information in his memoir accompanying *The Richmond Examiner During the War, or the Writings of John M. Daniel* (New York: Arno Press, 1970).

Edward A. Pollard, who served with Daniel on the *Examiner* during the war and was as stridently pro-Southern at that time as Daniel, underwent a strange metamorphosis after the war. The story is told by Jack P. Maddex in *The Reconstruction of Edward A. Pollard* (Chapel Hill: Univ. of North Carolina Press, 1974).

The Cowardins, father and son, of the Richmond *Dispatch*, have been written about only sketchily, despite their significance in Virginia's journalistic world. The *National Cyclopedia of American Biography*, vol. II, pp. 51–52, has a quite useful article on James A. Cowardin, and *Men of Mark in Virginia*, vol. IV (Washington, D.C.: Men of Mark Publishing Co., 1908) has interesting material on both men. Also the obituary of James Cowardin in the *Dispatch* for November 22, 1882, and the accompanying editorial provide important information.

The principal source for the appraisal of George W. Bagby's

writings and career is Joseph Leonard King's *Dr. George William Bagby: A Study of Virginian Literature, 1850–1880* (New York: Columbia Univ. Press, 1927). Other valuable information is contained in introductions to his collected works by Thomas Nelson Page and Douglas Southall Freeman, both of which appear in the fourth edition of *The Old Virginia Gentleman and Other Sketches*; the biographical article by Edward S. Gregory in the first volume of *Sketches From the Miscellaneous Writings of Dr. George W. Bagby* (Richmond: Whittet & Shepperson, 1884) is also useful.

William E. Cameron is given comprehensive treatment in the chapter by Walter T. Calhoun and James Tice Moore in *The Governors of Virginia, 1860–1978*, ed. Edward Younger and James Tice Moore (Charlottesville: Univ. Press of Virginia, 1982). Additional information is to be found in Allen W. Moger's book.

John Hampden Chamberlayne's wartime experiences, including his observations on certain Richmond newspapers, are described in his letters from the front, in *Ham Chamberlayne—Virginian*, ed. Churchill G. Chamberlayne (Richmond: Dietz Press, 1932). The introduction by the editor gives significant facts concerning his career, journalistic and otherwise. Further information is to be found in *Salt Water and Printer's Ink*, cited above.

William C. Elam's tempestuous course in journalism as spokesman for William Mahone is dealt with in *William Mahone of Virginia* by Nelson M. Blake (Richmond: Garrett & Massie, 1935), and also in the previously cited writings of Allen W. Moger, Charles C. Pearson, Charles E. Wynes, and Lenoir Chambers. Mahone is comprehensively examined in the aforementioned biography by Nelson M. Blake.

John Mitchell, Jr.'s life is exhaustively reviewed by Ann F. Alexander in "Black Protest in the New South: John Mitchell, Jr., and the Richmond *Planet*" (Ph.D. diss., Duke Univ., 1973). His banking career is analyzed by Abram L. Harris in *The Negro as Capitalist* (American Academy of Political and Social Science, 1936).

Some of Mitchell's furious attacks on the establishment are described in J. K. B. Williams, *Changed Views and Unforeseen Prosperity: Richmond of 1890 Gets a Monument to Lee* (Richmond, privately printed, 1969).

The principal source on the career of Joseph Bryan in all its phases is John Stewart Bryan's *Joseph Bryan: His Times, His Family, His Friends* (Richmond: Whittet & Shepperson, 1935). Allen W. Moger's book, cited above, is helpful as to Bryan's attitude toward crooked elections in Virginia and William Jennings Bryan's free silver crusade.

William L. Royall's *Some Reminiscences* (New York: Neale Publishing Co., 1909) sheds light on various happenings in the period.

Information and sidelights concerning events and controversies in the antebellum and postbellum eras may be found in Virginius Dabney's *Virginia: The New Dominion* (Garden City: Doubleday, 1971), and *Richmond: The Story of a City* (Garden City: Doubleday, 1976).